T3-BQR-242

J. E. Peterson

Saudi Arabia and the Illusion of Security

DISCARDED BY

MACPHÁIDÍN LIBRARY

Adelphi Paper 348

MACPHÁIDÍN LIBRARY
STONEHILL COLLEGE
EASTON, MASSACHUSETTS 02357

Oxford University Press, Great Clarendon Street, Oxford OX2 6DP
Oxford New York
Athens Auckland Bangkok Bombay Calcutta Cape Town
Dar es Salaam Delhi Florence Hong Kong Istanbul Karachi
Kuala Lumpur Madras Madrid Melbourne Mexico City
Nairobi Paris Singapore Taipei Tokyo Toronto
and associated companies in
Berlin Ibadan

Oxford is a trade mark of Oxford University Press

Published in the United States
by Oxford University Press Inc., New York

© The International Institute for Strategic Studies 2002

First published July 2002 by **Oxford University Press** for
The International Institute for Strategic Studies
Arundel House, 13–15 Arundel Street, Temple Place, London WC2R 3DX
www.iiss.org

Director John Chipman
Editor Mats R. Berdal
Assistant Editor John Wheelwright
Production Shirley Nicholls

All rights reserved. No part of this publication may be reproduced, stored in a
retrieval system or transmitted in any form or by any means, electronic, mech-
anical or photo-copying, recording or otherwise, without the prior permission of
The International Institute for Strategic Studies. Within the UK, exceptions are
allowed in respect of any fair dealing for the purpose of research or private
study, or criticism or review, as permitted under the Copyright, Designs and
Patents Act, 1988, or in the case of reprographic reproduction in accordance with
the terms of the licences issued by the Copyright Licensing Agency. Enquiries
concerning reproduction outside these terms and in other countries should be
sent c/o Permissions, Journals Department, Oxford University Press, Great
Clarendon Street, Oxford, OX2 6DP, UK.

This book is sold subject to the condition that it shall not, by way of trade or
otherwise, be lent, re-sold, hired out or otherwise circulated without the
publisher's prior consent in any form of binding or cover other than that in which
it is published and without a similar condition including this condition being
imposed on the subsequent purchaser.

British Library Cataloguing in Publication Data
Data available

Library of Congress Cataloguing in Publication Data

ISBN 0-19-851677-0
ISSN 0567-932x

Contents

Introduction

It is a truism that, for much of the world, the Gulf has been a central strategic consideration for decades.[1] A perceived Soviet threat to the region, the rise of Arab nationalism, the Iranian Revolution and the two 'Gulf Wars' – the Iran–Iraq War and the Kuwait War of Liberation – have all contributed to Western concern and military, as well as political, involvement. Furthermore, the terrorist attacks of 11 September 2001 on New York and Washington have intensified Western, and particularly American, worries about the Gulf and its surrounding region. Saudi Arabia was particularly embarrassed, distressed and threatened by the involvement of its nationals in the attacks. The attacks exposed the internal contradictions between a developing, modernist state and an undercurrent of strongly conservative Islamic tradition; they put the Kingdom under a strong and largely negative international spotlight; and they threatened to disrupt significantly both official and informal relations with the United States.

There are many reasons why the Kingdom of Saudi Arabia is a pivotal state for Western interests. Its position as the world's largest oil exporter is the most obvious, but the Kingdom's role as a moderating force in Arab politics and its moral status as a leader of the Islamic world are important too. In addition, Saudi Arabia is the fulcrum of the Gulf Cooperation Council (GCC).[2] The similarity of GCC members' internal politics, economics and societies, their regional security interests and their relationships with the West dictate that any analysis of Saudi Arabia's security framework must also take account of the role of its GCC allies.

Although Saudi Arabia has been at the core of Western strategic planning and preparation for contingencies affecting the Gulf, the Kingdom and its GCC allies essentially have been bystanders in the conceptualisation of Gulf security policy. Their acquiescence in Western designs and activities owes as much to state weakness and narrowly defined regime interests as to rational conceptions of genuine national security interests.

Weakness of regimes does not automatically translate into instability of states – the often-heard reservation of Western policy pundits. Outsiders have so often declared the Gulf monarchies obsolete – at the time of the rise of Arab socialism, the revolution in Iraq, the threat of pan-Arab nationalism, the civil war in Yemen, the intensification of Islamic radicalism and the revolution in Iran, and the segmentation of Arab politics and the invasion of Kuwait – yet they have survived and still endure. All the same, the effect of socio-economic changes on political structures is both immense and increasingly likely to produce serious challenges to the way these states operate. The internal dimension of Gulf security is generally overlooked, even though in the long run it may well prove to be the most important determinant of security.

The security of Saudi Arabia and its fellow Gulf states is increasingly becoming an illusion. Although direct threats from external sources have abated or are held in check, the events of late 2001 demonstrate that worrying cracks are appearing in the foundations of the present conception of Gulf security. First, there are growing differences with the United States over such issues as Israel/Palestine, Iraq, Iran, military and anti-terrorism cooperation, Saudi membership of the World Trade Organisation, and increasingly negative popular perceptions on each side. Second, the appearance of deep-rooted radical Islamist activism in Saudi Arabia puts an already fragile social fabric under extra stress. The first problem is likely to persist through the life of the Bush administration, and may well grow worse during this period. The second is even more intractable, and its precise effects will depend closely on the course of political change in Saudi Arabia and its neighbours.

Two fundamental questions must be asked at the outset: why is Saudi Arabia important and what is important in Saudi Arabia?

Why is Saudi Arabia important?

Answering the first question requires an understanding of why

Saudi Arabia is the central axis around which Western conceptions of Gulf security revolve.

Geopolitical situation

The Kingdom of Saudi Arabia is the largest and most powerful state in the Arabian Peninsula. Geographically, it lies at the crossroads of Middle Eastern security. On the one hand, it is a key Gulf player because of its important presence in the Gulf, its association with the smaller Gulf monarchies and the location of its oilfields near the Gulf. On the other hand, its western boundary is the Red Sea and it has a long, porous land border with Yemen, which forces the Kingdom to be involved in Yemeni, Red Sea and Horn of Africa affairs. To the north, the country borders the Fertile Crescent, which gives rise to complicated entanglement in northern Arab politics. This, combined with its quest for legitimacy in Arab affairs and its physical proximity to Israel, make the Kingdom an important, if reticent, actor in Arab–Israeli matters.

Saudi oil

The Kingdom is arguably the world's most important actor in oil affairs. Its crude oil production during December 2001 was an estimated 7.7 million barrels per day (mbd), down from a high of 8.9 mbd in November and December 2000. This constituted nearly 30% of the OPEC total of 25.86 mbd.[3] Throughout the 1990s Saudi production averaged well over 8 mbd, or roughly 13% of total world production,[4] and in 2000 the Kingdom was the United States' second-largest supplier of crude oil, with its 14% share ranking between Canada's and Venezuela's.[5] More recently, it has become the largest supplier. At the end of 1999 Saudi Arabia's reserves equalled 261.7 billion barrels of crude oil: 25% of the world's total of 1,046.4 trillion barrels.[6] The Kingdom is likely to maintain this proportion of reserves well into the next several decades.

America's regional ally and partner

For thirty years or more, Saudi Arabia has served as an important regional ally and partner of the United States. American oil companies founded the Saudi oil industry and played a key role in the country's early development, and the Kingdom is a major consumer of American products and services; it also plays an important role as America's partner in the Gulf and a moderating influence within Arab politics. Saudi Arabia has long been a major exporter of oil to the United States, Europe and Japan. (Asia and the Far East have long been the biggest regional destination, accounting in 1998 for 971.4m barrels, compared to 645.7m for Europe and 544.2m for North America.[7]) It has also long been a balancer within OPEC, and its principal goal has been to regulate OPEC production so as to maintain a steady, reasonable price. As the sole OPEC producer with significant excess capacity,[8] it has appeared in recent years to be returning to the role it last played in the 1980s as the organisation's 'swing producer'.

Influence on the region and Islam

Saudi Arabia exerts a significant role and influence in an overlapping series of regional and Islamic arenas. It dominates the Arabian Peninsula (consisting of the other five GCC states plus Yemen). It has been a principal supporter of Jordan, maintains close ties to Syria, and brokered the accord that essentially brought an end to the Lebanese civil war. The Kingdom is home to Islam's holiest sites, and it feels it exercises a special responsibility for the welfare of Islam everywhere. Since 11 September 2001, Saudi Arabia's role has been seen also in a more negative light, as the birthplace of Osama bin Laden and a recruiting ground for dozens, if not hundreds, of his supporters.

Linchpin of the GCC

The Kingdom is, by far, the dominant power within the GCC and thus the linchpin of the organisation. The GCC secretariat is located in Riyadh, the majority of its staff is composed of Saudis, and until March 2002 the post of GCC Secretary-General was held by a Saudi.

Influence on Arab–Israeli affairs

Riyadh has always shunned direct contacts with Israel and has been a staunch supporter of Arab positions and Palestinian rights. Yet the Kingdom has also sought to play a moderating role in Arab politics, to promote the prospects of peace, and to persuade its Arab allies to keep open channels for negotiation.

What is important in Saudi Arabia?

The second basic question concerns the composition of the Saudi state and society; how developments within the country are regarded; how the outside world is viewed; and what determines requirements and responses to the looming challenge of Gulf security.

Change in economy and society

The Kingdom has made massive efforts to advance socio-economic development in the past few decades, with expenditures of $1.285 trillion over the period between 1970/1971 and 1999.[9] Oil income has allowed a modern physical infrastructure for the country to be implemented and a social welfare net to be created for nearly all the population. The result has been a dramatic improvement in living standards and quality of life for most Saudis.

But economic transformation necessarily also results in social change. Advances in health care have resulted in a rapidly growing – and increasingly younger – population. The expanded educational system produces large numbers of young Saudi men and women unable to find employment; Saudis have replaced many of the expatriates in skilled positions, but the society has remained dependent on a legion of foreign workers in menial occupations. At a more profound level, family, tribal, and regional ties have loosened, as many Saudis have become urbanised and middle-class.

Stirrings of political change

Naturally, these economic and social changes have engendered pressures for political change. For many Saudis, this may represent little more than grumbling about what they see as threats to their share of the economic pie. On the one hand, they protest at the state's attempt to trim subsidies, because it lowers their standard of living. On the other, they object to the greed and extravagance of the ruling family and other elites, because they know that the pie is shrinking.

More significant political dissatisfaction tends to derive from opposite poles. There is a stubborn, arch-conservative, religious-based opposition that decries changes to the 'traditional' way, opposes the creeping 'Westernisation' of the country and attacks the hypocrisy of the royal family and allied elites. At the other end of the spectrum modernist, educated elements seek not just economic but also political liberalisation, including a rule by law, some degree of formal political participation and debate, and restrictions on the privileged status of the royal family.

Internal change and external relationships

The outside world views Saudi Arabia as primarily a Gulf state and the leader of the GCC. However, this is not how many – perhaps most – Saudis see their country. Perhaps predictably, the most important consideration for most Saudis is the country's internal differences and cohesion. Saudi Arabia's regions exhibit as much or more variation as can be found in the rest of the GCC combined and the country's boundaries are more encompassing than those of its GCC neighbours. Hence, the workings and future of the GCC may not be uppermost in many Saudi minds, as is the case elsewhere in the GCC and in the perceptions of Western observers.

Neither the Saudi regime nor its people regard the state's alliance with the West with equanimity. Even the Saudi leadership has become increasingly vocal about policy divergences. As time goes on, it is likely that most Saudis – whether the Islamic right, the educated liberals, or the great silent and 'apolitical' majority – will become more critical of the Western alliance and less supportive, albeit for different reasons. This trend became more pronounced in late 2001 and early 2002.

The impact of 11 September on Saudi policies

Many Saudis have been shocked to discover the role of 15 Saudis in the September hijackings and the involvement of hundreds more in al-Qaeda. Neither the government nor the citizenry can ever again be complacent about the appeal of radical Islam to Saudis across a wide spectrum. Equally, however, many Saudis have been offended at the way their country has been characterised in the West and especially the United States. While the mutually beneficial foundations of continuing strong Saudi–American partnership in many fields remain unshaken, the window of mutual mistrust has been opened wider. Externally, Saudi policy regarding the Taliban regime in Afghanistan ended ignominiously, and differences with Washington over Palestine and Iraq remain as sharp as ever. More than ever, the central Saudi creed of Wahabism is regarded with suspicion outside the Kingdom, and it is unlikely that Saudi Arabia will be able to regard itself so authoritatively as the protector of Islam in the foreseeable future.

Towards a viable Saudi strategy for Gulf security

A principal contention of this essay is that Western conceptions of

Gulf security do not accurately address the needs and concerns of the Gulf states. In fact, a fully developed, rational, Gulf conception of Gulf security may be diametrically opposed to the guiding principles of Western policy.

Western policy concerning Gulf security is predicated at least in part on protecting interests in Saudi Arabia and the other states of the GCC. Western policy also depends heavily on the cooperation of these states in carrying out its Gulf security goals. But does Western policy actually serve the interests of the Saudi state, the regime and/ or the people?

The governments of the West and Saudi Arabia share the view that the essence of Gulf security is the protection of oil – its production, transport and sale at a stable and reasonable price. Since the collapse of the Soviet Union, Western policy has centred on maintaining Gulf security by containing Iraq and Iran, and the West has persuaded the Saudis to cooperate with this policy on the basis that it assures their own protection. Saudi Arabia, though, only partly shares the premise about containing Iraq and Iran; Riyadh acquiesces in the Western definition and cooperates with Western policy arrangements for reasons of alliance maintenance and regime survival. Saudi and other Gulf citizens, however, are increasingly sceptical that Gulf security depends on an alliance with the West that is designed to contain Iraq and Iran. Many object to close ties with the United States, because of the perceived American role in causing the plight of the Iraqi people, and because of perceived American connivance with Israel. Many believe that the United States and the West exaggerate the dangers from Iraq and Iran in order to sell arms at inflated prices to Saudi Arabia and the Gulf states. Some even believe that the United States and the West are deliberately prolonging the international quarantine of Iraq in order to sell more arms and keep the Gulf states dependent on the West. There is widespread, if naive, belief that Osama bin Laden is a hero for standing up to the West (there was a nearly identical reaction to Saddam Hussein's defiance of the West in 1990).

Growing numbers of people in Saudi Arabia regard internal developments and challenges as the most serious threats to Gulf security. They argue that effective and durable policy towards Iraq and Iran must be based on inclusion rather than exclusion. Furthermore, the divergence within the Kingdom between regime and popular views of Gulf security threatens to drive a wedge between rulers and ruled. Debate about Gulf security, which potentially could lead to the formulation of a Saudi concept of Gulf security, is non-existent because the government inhibits free speech and resists meaningful political participation.

Chapter 1

Saudi conceptions of national and Gulf security

Western and GCC governments share the view that the essence of Gulf security is protecting oil – its production, transport and sale at a stable and reasonable price. This has been the cornerstone of Western and American policy-making since the Carter Doctrine and before. Just as importantly, even as Gulf oil is the lifeblood of the industrialised world, so oil revenues are the principal source of income for Gulf governments and the mainstay of their economic health.

But how can this objective be successfully achieved in what often seems to be an especially hostile environment? And, more to the point, how can this primary objective be squared with the strategy of containing Iraq and Iran that the West has pursued in the Gulf for the past decade? It should not be surprising that the views of Western governments and Gulf regimes on optimal Gulf security differ, particularly over the details, or that, on occasion, these differences may lead to friction, despite agreement on broad objectives.

Western conceptions of Gulf security have evolved into a primary objective of 'Gulf defence': the military capability to defend regional interests and friendly states. But, as American and other Western states increased their power projection in the region, the emphasis shifted from confronting a Soviet threat to facing regional threats to Western interests. By the 1990s the perceived threats had narrowed down to Iraq and Iran, and the Clinton administration's Gulf policy was articulated as 'dual containment'. The second Bush administration retained the same policy, characterising these two states (along with North Korea) as an 'axis of evil'. The short-term purpose of containment seemed to be to minimise the damage that both states could cause to Western interests and Western clients. In the longer term, containment seemed to be intended to force change in regime policies, and even in regimes themselves. In particular, after the American military victory in Afghanistan, the Bush administration's frustration with Saddam Hussein's continued rule in Baghdad provoked more bellicose calls for 'regime change' in Iraq.

Saudi Arabia and the Gulf monarchies are at once the objects of Western protection and partners in the Western scheme of Gulf security. However, they have a decidedly secondary status in the partnership, and generally are expected to do little more than accept, approve and implement Western ideas and actions. Since both parties have separate agendas, which sometimes conflict, it is not surprising that this partnership periodically comes under serious strain. If it is to remain strong and viable, then a core aspect of the partnership must be that it should accommodate Saudi Arabia's perceptions of its security requirements.

Saudi security perceptions include many geopolitical constants, but they have not been immutable; they have reflected changes in political circumstances over the past several decades. For example, during the 1980s Iran and the Soviet Union constituted perhaps the most serious threats to Saudi security, while Iraq was a bulwark that deserved support against the menace of the Islamic republic. A decade later the Soviet threat, the driving force behind so much of Western planning for Gulf security, disappeared and had been replaced by the Iraqi threat, which has assumed similar ominous proportions in Western eyes; meanwhile, Riyadh has pursued a successful rapprochement with Tehran. For all that, though, divergence of opinion between the Gulf states and the West over Israel's role in the region continues unabated, and, since the outbreak of the second *intifada* or Palestinian unrest in late 2000, it has become even sharper.

The difficulty of Saudi Arabia's position is that it appears to be surrounded by real or potential enemies, most of whom are bigger and more powerful. Thus the Kingdom must tread warily with its neighbours, using all its skills of diplomacy and consensus-building, while forging strong alliances with dependable powers. The country has dealt with the perceived multitude of threats by creating armed forces to protect its oilfields and territory. But, given the limitations on its military power, even greater emphasis has been placed on a foreign policy that includes financial inducements and moral weight, along with close coordination and alliance with the Arab and Islamic world, the GCC and the West. The following pages outline Riyadh's perceived external threats and then discuss the Kingdom's strategies for dealing with them.

Saudi security horizons: regional threat assessments
Iran

Iran has always been a source of worry to the Saudi state. In part, this is because of ancient Arab–Persian suspicions in the Gulf, compounded by Wahabi views of Iran's Shiite faith. While relations were correct during the reign of Shah Muhammad Reza Shah, and the two countries served as the foundations of the United States' twin-pillar strategy, age-old suspicions remained.

The Iranian Revolution of 1978–9 disrupted relations tremendously and ushered in a long period of animosity. During the 1980s low points in the relationship were reached with the Saudi shooting down of an Iranian F-4 combat aircraft in 1984, Iranian attacks on Saudi shipping during the 'tanker war' aspect of the latter stages of the Iran–Iraq War, the Iranian demonstration during the 1987 *haj* (Islamic pilgrimage) that left hundreds dead, and bombs set off by Iranian agents during the 1989 *haj*. But through the 1990s relations gradually improved. Crown Prince Abdullah met Iranian President Muhammad Khatami during the 1997 Organisation of Islamic Conference summit in Tehran; former Iranian President Akbar Hashemi Rafsanjani visited the Kingdom early the following year; and Khatami went to Saudi Arabia in 1999. More significantly, the two countries began discussing a security pact in early 2000, and in April 2001 Prince Nayif bin Abd al-Aziz became the first Saudi Interior Minister to visit Iran since the revolution, when he travelled to Tehran to sign the agreement – described as an instrument for cooperation in the joint surveillance of borders and in combating organised crime, terrorism, drug trafficking and illegal immigration.

Events in Iran, and the republic's activities outside its borders, have preoccupied Saudi leaders for more than two decades. Only in the last few years have they concluded that stability seems to exist in Iran and recognised that there is no alternative to the present system. They have improved relations with Tehran because they see realistic possibilities for removing Iranian antipathy to Saudi Arabia and its place in the world, thereby ending both Iran's support for terrorism as a way to subvert the Kingdom and its efforts to foment trouble amongst the Saudi Shiite minority, and moderating the Iranian drive for leadership of the Islamic world.

The Saudi leaders believe that Iran is going through a natural evolution as a state. As it evolves, it becomes easier to deal with on key issues, in part because it is easier to deal with President Khatami – to speak frankly and to reach agreement with him. They believe that Khatami is a genuine reformer, with a broader, more realistic world view than previous Iranian presidents, and that he recognises that Iran must change its ways and reach a *modus vivendi* with its neighbours and world powers in order to survive and grow. They are also encouraged by the improvement in Iran's relations with Bahrain and Kuwait in recent years, although continued Iranian occupation of the Gulf islands of Abu Musa and the two Tunbs continues to cause problems with the United Arab Emirates, and thus with the GCC.

There are still serious reasons for Riyadh to worry, however. First, there is the question of Khatami's position in Iran's politics: even after his re-election by an overwhelming margin in June 2001, the likelihood of his forcing the conservatives to retreat, or even of simply holding his ground, seem very slim. In addition, Saudi Arabia remains very concerned with Iran's military potential, particularly its acquisition of weapons of mass destruction (WMD). Official assurances from Tehran that Iran is not building a nuclear bomb are not believed in Riyadh, in part because it continues to see the regime as inherently antagonistic and in part because Tehran clearly believes that it is being targeted and impinged upon by the great powers.

Iraq

For nearly half a century Saudi Arabia has viewed Iraq with suspicion. For several decades after the 1958 Iraqi revolution, the Kingdom – like its fellow monarchies – was an Iraqi target, as shown by Baghdad's support for sabotage and opposition fronts. Riyadh's alliance with Saddam Hussein during the Iran–Iraq War of 1980–88 came about not so much because common interests had emerged as because Saudi Arabia feared the intentions of the revolutionary regime in Iran more than those of Iraq.

The underlying Saudi suspicions of Saddam Hussein's true character and intentions were abruptly revived in August 1990, with the Iraqi invasion of Kuwait. This, of course, drew the Kingdom even closer to the United States, because of the new requirements for protection against what had become a very real Iraqi threat. The Kingdom contributed to the war to free Kuwait by providing access facilities for coalition forces on Saudi territory, by contributing to and providing the overall leadership for Arab elements of those coalition forces, and by organising Arab and Islamic support for the cause. After Kuwait's liberation, Riyadh supported all UN resolutions on Iraq, including the sanctions regime and no-fly zones. Its support for the last, in particular, was crucial because of the basing of American, British and – for a time – French aircraft on Saudi soil. However, this support became troublesome for Saudi Arabia because of the widespread criticism and even condemnation that it attracted, particularly after the sanctions regime entered its second decade without any realistic prospect of the underlying problem being resolved.

How do the Saudis view Iraq now and in the future? First, as a close neighbour, Iraq is regarded as intrinsically of great interest, for the two countries are linked by common ethnic, historical and religious backgrounds. Riyadh desperately wishes to see an end to the negative developments since the liberation of Kuwait, but realises that, by itself, it has little power to affect events.

While acknowledging that the United States has taken the lead in confronting Iraq, Saudi Arabia insists that certain ground rules apply:

1.   Iraq must remain united in territory and geography;
2.   It must become a stable and sound neighbour in the area and contribute to security and stability;
3.   Only the people of Iraq can decide their own future – there should be no imposition from the outside; and
4.   Saudi Arabia cannot deal with Saddam Hussein, since he betrayed both Saudi trust and its values.

Riyadh maintains that the Kingdom will not interfere in Iraq, though it agrees that the sooner Saddam Hussein is removed, the sooner stability will be restored. Furthermore, Saudi Arabia is not convinced that Iraq's WMD capability has been destroyed and, as a neighbour and potential target, it insists upon a means of identifying and controlling such capability. There is evidence of some frustration with American policy. The policy of dual containment, it is thought, gave the initiative to Saddam, and he has exploited humanitarian concerns over the effects of the embargo on the Iraqi people.

Riyadh supports any measure to alleviate suffering of the Iraqi people, but at the same time believes that Saddam's emphasis on the plight of his people means that he does not want the embargo to be removed – it provides him with external support and keeps his own people hostage to the West and thus dependent on him. Saddam has also cleverly exploited the continued coalition bombing of Iraq and the second *intifada* as ammunition to be used against the West – and thus against the Kingdom, because of its close cooperation with the West.

The big question is, how long Saddam will stay in power? Having ruled out its own intervention to overthrow him, Saudi Arabia seems to pin its hopes on natural death or a successful coup.[1] In its eyes, Saddam's eldest son Uday is little different from his father, uncontrolled and impulsive, and the Saudi stance towards Iraq would remain unchanged if Uday took over. On the other hand, the Saudis seem more amenable to working with the younger son Qusay if necessary, regarding him as more stable and reliable.

Pakistan

Saudi Arabia has enjoyed close ties with Pakistan since the latter's creation in 1947. Pakistan is strategically important to the Kingdom for a number of reasons. First, it has one of the largest populations of all Islamic countries. Second, thousands of Pakistanis live and work in the Kingdom. Third, its Makran coast sits at the entrance to the Gulf, not far from the Strait of Hormuz. Fourth, in addition to providing military assistance to the Kingdom (especially in seconding skilled personnel for the Saudi navy and air force), Pakistan is regarded as one of the bulwarks of Islam against its worldwide enemies. The potential role of Pakistan's nuclear capability as an 'Islamic bomb' has generated considerable speculation, and it has been conjectured that Riyadh sees the Pakistani nuclear arsenal as a useful counter to Iran's aspirations in the same direction.[2]

Another factor in the close relationship is the personal ties between the Al Saud and various Pakistani leaders.[3] Pakistani Prime

Minister Nawaz Sharif publicly admitted that in 1998, after India had exploded its nuclear devices and before Pakistan responded, he had consulted the leaders of Saudi Arabia and the UAE; and Crown Prince Abdullah made a high-profile visit to Pakistan a few months later to emphasise Saudi moral and financial support.[4] After General Pervez Musharraf seized power in 1999, his first trip abroad was to the Kingdom.[5] The Saudis subsequently lobbied Musharraf to commute the death sentence levied on his predecessor Nawaz Sharif and agreed to give the exiled Sharif and his family refuge in the Kingdom.[6]

At the same time, however, Pakistan is a source of potential problems. In part, this stems from its inclination towards internal fragmentation due to its four independent-minded provinces, serious Sunni–Shiite differences, the alienation of the *Mohajirs* (Muslims originally from India), especially in Karachi, corrupt civilian politics, and the repeated imposition of military rule. For the Kingdom the collapse, virtually next door, of one of the Islamic world's largest and most important states would have serious spill-over implications.

There are also troubling hiccups in the bilateral relationship, although they have not been big enough to shake its foundations. News reports in the mid-1980s spoke of 10,000–16,000 Pakistani soldiers stationed in Saudi Arabia, including a tank brigade at Tabuk in the north-west corner of the country. The ostensible purpose of the tanks was to provide defence against Israel, but Pakistan's refusal to allow the troops to be transferred to Saudi Arabia's front-line defences against Iran, particularly after the June 1987 *haj* riots, supposedly resulted in Riyadh terminating the contractual arrangements for the use of the troops, and they were sent home. It was also alleged that Pakistan refused a Saudi demand that the Shiite element of the Pakistani troops (said to be 10–15% of the total) be sent home. Riyadh, however, insisted that the Pakistani troops were being sent home because their contractual term had expired and there was no more need for them.[7] Shortly afterwards, relations were momentarily jarred when the Saudis arrested a number of Pakistani (and other) Shiite activists during the 1988 *haj*.[8]

In addition, Islamabad's rocky relations with its immediate neighbours raise the potential for conflict in the vicinity of Saudi Arabia. Pakistani relations with Iran have been troubled by persistent Sunni–Shiite violence – with radical Sunni groups assassinating Shiite targets in Pakistan, and Iran allegedly sponsoring retaliation against

Sunni figures there. The Pakistani military, particularly through its Inter-Services Intelligence (ISI) agency, was a principal actor in the formation and training of the Taliban movement in Afghanistan. (Until the American intervention in Afghanistan, there were abundant allegations of continued ISI connections with the Taliban – and even, through the Taliban, with Islamic radicals in Central Asia). These ISI activities have been of direct concern to Saudi Arabia because of the Kingdom's ambivalent relationship with the Taliban and Riyadh's concern over certain aspects of Islamic radicalisation in Central Asia.

And, in the other direction, Pakistani–Indian relations have been a flashpoint for over 50 years. India's detonation of its first atomic device in 1998, shortly followed by a similar test by Pakistan, threatened to raise the stakes in another war between the two states, but fortunately the disaster was averted. Equally vexatious is the issue of Kashmir, with the Pakistani military accused of actively supporting Kashmiri separatists in violent anti-Indian activities.[9] The Saudis support Pakistan on the question of Kashmir and back UN resolutions on the region because they feel the situation is very similar to that of Palestine, but, similarly, they realise that a peaceful resolution in Kashmir is unlikely for the foreseeable future.

Afghanistan

Even more than the West, Saudi Arabia was dismayed by the Russian occupation of Afghanistan in 1979. While it fully shared the West's anti-Communist objections to the puppet government, it carried the additional concern of seeking an appropriate response to an attack upon the Islamic world. The Saudis supported Afghani resistance groups financially[10] and sought to create a moderate coalition to serve as a government-in-exile. In addition, thousands of Saudis went to Afghanistan to fight against the Soviet occupation.[11] Along with Pakistan, Saudi Arabia brokered the reconciliation agreement signed in Mecca between the leading factions in 1993.[12]

When that agreement failed, and the Taliban extended their control, Saudi Arabia provided important financial support to the Taliban. It was, with Pakistan and the UAE, one of the only three countries to recognise the Taliban as rulers of Afghanistan. But relations with the movement soon soured.[13] In large part, this appeared to be due to the granting of asylum to Osama bin Laden in

Afghanistan in 1996. Bin Laden's contribution to the struggle against the Russians had been welcomed both in Afghanistan and by the Saudi government. However, as the extreme radicalism of his views became clear, an embarrassed Riyadh revoked his citizenship and eventually downgraded its diplomatic presence in Kabul in 1998, in protest at the Taliban's extreme interpretation of Islam and particularly their refusal to hand over bin Laden.[14] The Saudis, however, continued to support mediation between the Taliban and their Afghan opponents, hosting talks in the Kingdom in 2000.[15] In the end, it was clear that the Kingdom had overestimated its influence on the Taliban and underestimated bin Laden's impact. Saudi Foreign Minister Prince Saud al-Faisal remarked 'The stability of Afghanistan seemed a bigger concern than the presence of bin Laden. When the Taliban received him, they indicated he would be absolutely prevented from taking any actions. We had unequivocal promises.'[16]

Although the Saudis were particularly embarrassed by Osama bin Laden's apparent orchestration of the attacks of 11 September, and the Saudi government quickly stated its approval of American actions against bin Laden, it viewed the invasion of Afghanistan with disquiet.[17] Riyadh may have regarded the dénouement of the war with some relief, provided American anti-terrorist activity did not continue against other Islamic countries, but it certainly could not have viewed a new Afghan government dominated by the Northern Alliance with equanimity. Additional embarrassment resulted from the fact that Saudi citizens were involved in the 11 September attacks and were among the members of al-Qaeda captured in Afghanistan. Nevertheless, interim Afghan President Hamid Karzai made Saudi Arabia the destination of his first official visit and received an initial pledge of $20m in urgent aid, with a further commitment of $200m made at the January donors' meeting in Tokyo.[18]

The Northern Arab States

These states no longer pose the sort of threat they did a few decades ago, when Nasserist Egypt and Ba'athist Syria and Iraq demanded and schemed for the overthrow of the Al Saud and other monarchical systems in the region. Saudi Arabia has proved as durable as its erstwhile adversaries, if not more so. Still, even if it is no longer faces an ideological threat from this quarter, it remains on guard against the resentment expressed by poorer populations, many of whom work in Saudi Arabia.

Indirectly, relations with northern Arab states pose the potential hazard of divergence on pan-Arab issues – such as relations with the United States – which has implications for Saudi Arabia's leadership role within the Arab world. The Kingdom has indisputably sought to play an active and influential role in Arab councils. The desire to present an Arab point of view was perhaps a primary motivation for King Abd al-Aziz's meeting with President Roosevelt during the Second World War. However, given its relatively small population, modest industrial base and limited military power, the status Saudi Arabia enjoys in inter-Arab councils depends on financial largesse, moral reputation and leverage with the United States.

With the ending of the Arab Cold War in the late 1960s, Saudi stock rose in the Arab world, particularly as its conduct of foreign policy grew more sophisticated. Still, many of the determinants of Riyadh's Arab policies have been weakened in recent years. The decline in nominal oil prices in the last decade – compounded by their declining value in real terms to a level lower than the price in 1974 – combines with growing domestic demands on the Saudi budget to limit the amount of largesse available. (In addition, the Kingdom's disbursements bring a rather poor return in influence, because of the Saudi custom of handing out monies with insufficient controls over their use.) Furthermore, the Kingdom's moral claim, based on its role as protector of Islam's holiest sites, has come under increasing attack by Islamic radicals. Finally, the 'special relationship' Saudi Arabia enjoys with the United States is seen by many more as a liability than an asset.

On almost any issue, the Arab world is no closer to joint action than it was at the founding of the Arab League over 50 years ago. Therefore, the scope for pan-Arab political cooperation remains minimal, as does Saudi Arabia's role in such an arena. And if political cooperation is minimal at best, then it stands to reason that military cooperation is even less likely. Moreover, while Riyadh sees political cooperation is a desirable goal, it has strong reservations about closer military ties. Token Saudi troops have served on the Arab–Israeli front, but the closest the Kingdom has come to significant military cooperation occurred when Egyptian and Syrian troops were dispatched to fight with coalition forces – alongside

GCC forces and under the nominal command of a Saudi general –
during the Kuwait War. But those troops returned home after the
hostilities ended, and it seems that this alliance was only a short-
term tactical response; the pursuit of a more robust and permanent
partnership does not seem feasible in the foreseeable future.[19] The
threats to Saudi security from the northern Arab direction, insofar as
they exist, are indirect and related to its standing within the Arab
world and its relationship with the United States.

Israel, Palestine and Arab–Israeli conflict

Although small numbers of Saudi troops have been stationed along
the borders with Israel and took part in some of the Arab–Israeli
Wars, the Kingdom has never been an Arab front-line state. There
has never been direct confrontation with Israel, although such
confrontation could have arisen out of incidental contact. Israel
occupied several Saudi islands in the Gulf of Aqaba during the 1956
War and again during the 1967 War, returning them to Egyptian
control (the *status quo ante*) in connexion with its withdrawal from
Sinai in 1982. In addition, Israeli aircraft are said to have overflown
Saudi airspace on a number of occasions.

    The possibility of direct Israeli attack or sabotage is unlikely,
given Saudi Arabia's history of non-confrontation and the limited
military threat that it poses. Still, Israel's WMD capabilities may play
a part in Saudi strategic perceptions, particularly at a time when
Israel's relations with its Arab neighbours are worsening. At the same
time, Israel and its supporters regard Saudi Arabia as a serious threat,
particularly because of its ties to the United States, and actively work
to undermine its position and relationship with Washington.

    Saudi–Palestinian relations are chronically troubled. The
Kingdom has always been doubtful (even fearful) of Palestinian
radicalism, whether embodied by ideologically leftist groups or,
more recently, by Islamic entities such as Hamas or Islamic Jihad.
While wholeheartedly supporting the principles of the Palestinian
cause, Saudi leadership in the past has been suspicious of Yasser
Arafat and his intentions and motivations (Palestinian–Saudi
relations suffered as a result of the Palestinian support for Iraq after
the invasion of Kuwait). Nevertheless, Saudi Arabia continues to
lobby the international community and the United States on behalf of
the Palestinian cause. It makes regular subventions to the Palestine

Liberation Organisation/Palestinian Authority and helped to create
the two special funds set up at an Arab summit after the outbreak of
the second *intifada* in October 2000, pledging to provide $250m of the
$1bn total.[20]

Yemen and the Horn of Africa

Yemen has been a source of worry to the Saudis since the Yemeni
Revolution of 1962.[21] The emergence of a Nasserist republic on the
Saudis' doorstep was unnerving, even without the presence of up to
50,000 Egyptian troops and the scattered incidents of Egyptian
bombing of Saudi territory during the civil war in Yemen (1962–67).
In the end, the Saudis were obliged to acquiesce in the status of the
Yemen Arab Republic, albeit without the Egyptian military presence,
in part because of the emergence of an even more radical state in
newly independent South Yemen. Between 1967 and 1990 Saudi
policy was uncertainly balanced between cautiously supporting the
moderate regimes in North Yemen (while often working behind the
scenes to ensure that they remained weak and divided) and
attempting to contain the Marxist regime in South Yemen. The
destructive effect of infighting within Aden's leadership and the
impact of the Soviet Union's collapse led South Yemen to offer to
merge with North Yemen in 1990. Saudi concern was redoubled over
the implications of a larger, more powerful and unified state, and
Riyadh gave tacit support to the southern secessionists during the
1994 civil war between the two parts of the country.

Relations between Saudi Arabia and Yemen continue to be
patchy for the same underlying reasons, although many outstanding
differences have been settled. Because the Yemen government
refused to condemn the Iraqi invasion of Kuwait in 1990, up to one
million Yemeni workers in Saudi Arabia were expelled. The
additional burden to Yemen of these workers combined with a
drastic shortfall in foreign economic assistance to create enormous
hardship for the country, which Saudi Arabia has only gradually
and partially helped to ameliorate. A welcome development was
resolution of the border dispute between the two countries in 1995.
With Yemeni acceptance at long last of permanent Saudi sovereignty
in the provinces over which it took control in 1934, the way was
open to completing tortuous negotiations over the demarcation of
the common border as defined in a treaty of 2000.

Although it is highly unlikely that Yemen would launch an unprovoked attack against its larger neighbour, the Kingdom remains concerned about the potential for internal fragmentation in Yemen, due to its poverty, the narrowness of its president's ruling base, the independent and armed nature of the tribes, and the presence in Yemen of Islamic extremists because of the regime's weakness.

Similar fears of instability and violence spilling over from the Horn of Africa are also among Saudi concerns. Although the war between Ethiopia and Eritrea has ground to a halt, the situation is not permanently settled. Furthermore, the fragmentation of and disarray in Somalia invites outside intervention in ways that may be antithetical to Saudi interests. The Kingdom is also concerned about the future of Sudan, both in terms of the stability of the regime in Khartoum and in the ramifications of the 30-year civil war between the Arab Muslim north and the Christian south.

Relations with GCC neighbours

For nearly two centuries before the formal establishment of the Kingdom of Saudi Arabia in 1932, the Al Saud marshalled their political and military resources to impose the Wahabi view of Islamic purification on as much of the Arabian Peninsula as they could, and occasionally beyond it.

Not surprisingly, this left a legacy of subconscious suspicion in the minds of most neighbours. Saudi incursions in the nineteenth century spread through most of what is now the United Arab Emirates (UAE) and deep into Oman. A lingering consequence was the crisis of 1952–5 when Saudi forces occupied the Buraimi oasis, claimed before and since by Abu Dhabi (one of the constituent members of the UAE) and Oman.[22] Poor relations with Kuwait resulted in a Saudi economic blockade early in the twentieth century, and the Kingdom took over much Kuwaiti-claimed territory through a 1922 treaty. The creation of British mandates for Jordan and Iraq prevented Saudi expansion to the north, and the British-protected status of the smaller Gulf states also insulated them against Saudi designs.

In some ways, therefore, it took extraordinary circumstances to bring Saudi Arabia and its Gulf neighbours together in the GCC. The first undoubtedly was the climate of aggressive Arab nationalism in the 1950s and 1960s. The second was the full independence of the Gulf states, beginning with Kuwait in 1961 and culminating with British withdrawal from the Gulf in 1971. The third was the Iranian Revolution in 1979, followed shortly by the eruption of the Iran–Iraq War. Not only did these latter events stoke the urgency that lay behind the creation of the GCC in February 1981, they also created the practical circumstances in which it was possible for the organisation to be created – by removing Iran and, especially, Iraq from consideration.

The consequence was a grouping of like-minded countries that sought to build closer integration in the economic and political arenas, as well as in regional security. In fact, the rhetoric and modest accomplishments of the first few years tended to ignore the question of security. The establishment of the Peninsula Shield Force at the Saudi base at Hafar al-Batin (in the north-east corner of the Kingdom) was meant as the forerunner of a more unified GCC response to Gulf security, but was never actually more than symbolic. Although rhetoric and regular joint and multilateral exercises extolled the virtues of military integration, very few real efforts were made. Most defensive preparations were made by individual countries through bilateral arms purchases and cooperative agreements with outside powers, chiefly the United States and Britain.

A principal reason for the failure of the GCC to integrate more in most spheres – not just regional security and military matters – lies in the inherent imbalance between Saudi Arabia and its five much smaller allies. The Kingdom estimates its population at more than 22m, while the total population of the other five combined is not likely to be more than 9m. The Saudi GDP of $185bn (in 2000) far outstrips the others' cumulative total of $128bn.[23] Thus, the historic fear of Saudi expansionism blends with present concerns about becoming submerged in a larger Saudi economy.

Such concerns and suspicions on the part of the smaller five are mirrored in the military sphere. Active Saudi Arabian armed forces personnel total about 126,500 (over 200,000 when active National Guard personnel are included), as against 147,000 for all the rest of the GCC, and estimated defence expenditures during 1999 were $18.7bn for Saudi Arabia and slightly over $10bn for the rest of the GCC.[24] The headquarters for the GCC is located in Riyadh, and the Assistant Secretary-General for Defence Affairs has always been a Saudi. Thus, while the Kingdom has viewed a joint GCC defence force with some enthusiasm, other GCC states have been reluctant to go along, for fear the force would be Saudi-dominated and Saudi-subservient. Similarly, some member states have accepted GCC-wide internal security agreements only grudgingly, bearing in mind instances of Saudi pressure on its neighbours to rein in and arrest citizens for actions or writings that Riyadh considered inflammatory.

Oil security and defence

Saudi Arabia's primary concern must be the protection of its oilfields, if not the lines of communication once the oil leaves the Kingdom. Protection of the oilfields, pipelines and terminals against sabotage and other internal disruption is relatively easy to achieve, and this is the responsibility of the National Guard, in support of Saudi ARAMCO oil company preparations. The oilfields and the pipelines are mostly located in uninhabited areas and are easily monitorable in desert conditions. The principal terminal is at Ras Tanura and is heavily guarded. Once crude oil is loaded onto tankers, however, Saudi defensive capabilities quickly diminish, and protecting the lines of communication becomes an international responsibility (just as ownership of most of the crude is no longer Saudi).

Saudi Arabia is a large country of about 2.2m square kilo-metres (by comparison, the United Kingdom is 243,500km², France 547,000km² , Pakistan 803,900km², Iran 1.6m km² and the United States 9.6m km²), much of it uninhabited or lightly inhabited desert. The Kingdom's oil facilities are concentrated in the Eastern Province, along the Gulf, which comprises one of three principal areas of defensive priority for the country. Besides containing the Kingdom's oil, the Eastern Province also encompasses the new urban conglomeration of Dammam/Dhahran, the traditional agricultural oases of al-Hasa and al-Qatif, and the industrial city of Jubayl.

The other two areas of high defence priority are the capital at Riyadh (the Kingdom's largest city) and the urban centres of al-Hijaz province, including the commercial hub of Jeddah, the holy cities of Mecca and Medina, and the city of Taif. These three areas, stretching across the Kingdom in an east–west band, are the focal point of Saudi defence arrangements. The distances between cities and military bases poses major challenges. Riyadh is 390km from Dammam on the Gulf and 950km from Jeddah on the Red Sea, and the distance from the southernmost city of Jizan to the northern provincial capital of Arar is nearly 2,250km.

Not surprisingly, the oldest components of the Saudi armed forces are the land forces. But as threats to the Kingdom evolved and became more sophisticated, the Kingdom's defensive priorities moved to the air force and air defence. The principal elements in the Saudi military structure are outlined below.

Formally, the High Defence Council determines policy, although in practice the King's decisions are final. The council was established in 1961, with membership consisting of the King, the Ministers of Defence and Aviation, Finance and National Economy, Communications, and Foreign Affairs, and the Chief-of-Staff. The Minister of Defence and Aviation (since 1962 the office has been occupied by Prince Sultan bin Abd al-Aziz, regarded as second in line for the throne) controls the army, air force and navy, while the National Guard (commanded by the Heir Apparent) theoretically falls under the control of the Minister of the Interior, along with the Frontier Force, the Coast Guard and internal security forces. In practice, however, the National Guard is answerable only to Crown Prince Abdullah.[25]

Royal Saudi Air Force

The air force has held pride of place in the Kingdom's military modernisation, in large part because the Kingdom's geography means that most attacks would have to be launched by air across the Red Sea, the Gulf or the northern and southern deserts. The distance from the northern and southern borders to the Kingdom's centres of population, industry and oilfields also provides strategic defence. The development of the air force has relied most on American assistance, beginning with the provision of fighters in the 1950s and transport aircraft in the 1960s. But, even though the relationship continued with high-profile purchases of F-5 and F-15 combat aircraft and AWACS radar aircraft in the 1970s and early 1980s, the political problems of getting F-14 and F-16 purchases through a pro-Israeli US Congress forced the Saudis to turn to Britain for *Tornado* aircraft. The air force remains the most professional and prestigious of the Saudi services.

Royal Saudi Land Forces

The army is the largest force, with some 75,000 personnel organised into nine brigades: three armoured, five mechanised and one airborne. Tank capabilities include 350 M-1A2 *Abrams* and 450 M-60A3s; the 290 AMX-30s are being relegated to storage. The army also employs large numbers of armoured personnel carriers, infantry fighting vehicles, self-propelled and towed artillery and a number of attack and support helicopters. Although it has heavier equipment than the National Guard, the army is said to lack manpower and leadership, and is organised to fight more from the military cities it utilises than to conduct rapid deployments.[26]

Royal Saudi Navy

This was one of the last of the armed forces to emerge, being formed as an adjunct of the army in 1957 and functioning as a separate force only from 1969. Over-ambitious programmes for its expansion were scaled back on several occasions, and it remains hampered by a lack of qualified manpower and a division of sources of equipment, training and concepts between the United States and France. With 15,500 personnel, including 3,000 marines, the navy boasts eight frigates and a number of missile and patrol craft, and operates out of bases on both the Red Sea and the Gulf.[27]

Royal Saudi Air Defence Forces

Air defence units were detached from the army in 1984 to form a fourth service under the initial command of Prince Khalid bin Sultan, son of the Minister of Defence and Aviation and the commander of Arab forces during the Kuwait War. Air defence forces number 16,000 men with 33 SAM batteries, 73 *Shahine/Crotale* missile fire units and Chinese ballistic missiles. The units are positioned to guard the country's main cities, industrial centres, air bases and oilfields and facilities.[28]

National Guard

The Saudi Arabian National Guard (SANG) originated as a tribal force providing armed might during King Abd al-Aziz's recon-stitution of the Saudi state early in the twentieth century. For many years the SANG was little more than a weak imitation of the army, receiving far fewer resources than other security forces and constituting a means for distributing income to loyal tribes. But a modernisation programme was initiated in 1972, with American assistance, to help the SANG accomplish its mission of maintaining internal security (as distinct from the army's mission of defending the country from external threats). About 75% of its total listed personnel of 100,000 are active, uniformed guardsmen, and professionalism and capabilities have increased markedly in recent years. Equipment consists largely of wheeled armoured infantry fighting vehicles and armoured personnel carriers, as well as some towed artillery. While the SANG's principal tasks include oil installation defence, counter-terrorism and handling civil disturbances, it is focusing increasingly on combat capabilities, including support for the army in hostile situations.[29]

Ministry of Interior

The Ministry of the Interior is the largest employer in the Saudi government with more than 500,000 employees, of whom some 160,000 are said to be directly employed in security.[30] Such paramilitary forces as the Frontier Force (10,500 personnel), the Coast Guard (4,500), the Public Security Police (20,000) and the Special Security Force (500) come under its control.[31]

Saudi foreign policy

There are serious inherent limitations to Saudi foreign policy. The country has a relatively small population and a proportionately small and weak military establishment. Therefore, the real strength of Saudi foreign policy has been in the traits of continuity, patience and persistence.

The Kingdom generally seeks to conduct its foreign policy and address its security concerns behind closed doors. It attempts to achieve an understanding, if not consensus, on disputes in much the same way that domestic politics are conducted. Relations with potentially threatening neighbours and other threats larger than Saudi defence capabilities are generally marked by subdued responses, hidden diplomacy and reliance on trustworthy allies for protection. Because of its small size, the Kingdom makes the most of such limited resources as financial rewards and moral suasion in its capacity as 'protector of the holy places'. Saudi relations with smaller neighbours, however, display a history of paradoxical behaviour, like that of a protective big brother who from time to time creates crises by insisting on having his own way on issues large and small.

Moral persuasion

This tool has obvious limitations. Riyadh may well seek to project an ethical voice in the Arab arena, but relying on such a strategy has many disadvantages. From a broader point of view, assuming an Islamic mantle may permit Saudi Arabia to exercise some degree of moral leadership in the Islamic arena, but it is a double-edged sword, leaving the Kingdom open to charges of hypocrisy for the ostentatiousness of its ruling family and to attacks on its harsh interpretation of Islam and its treatment of women and expatriate workers. Despite being a self-proclaimed Islamic state, the Kingdom is vulnerable to being outflanked in terms of Islamic conservatism by revisionist Muslim regimes and groups – inside the country as well as outside.

By and large, Saudi Arabia has been more willing to maintain or open relations with unfriendly powers than the reverse. It established diplomatic ties with Beijing in 1990, even though it has always been staunchly anti-communist and had decried Chinese backing for Marxist South Yemen and Omani rebels. The Chinese connexion has proved useful already, albeit in a roundabout way, when the Kingdom purchased several dozen DF-3 *East Wind* ballistic missiles adapted for conventional warheads, and thereby provoked a spat with the United States. Similarly, the Kingdom opened channels with Moscow well before the demise of the Soviet Union. The first tentative steps towards renewal of a lapsed relationship[32] were taken in the mid-1980s, driven partly by Saudi desire to persuade Moscow to exert its influence to moderate Iran's activities in the Iran–Iraq War. Full relations were not established until September 1990, despite Riyadh's misgivings about the Soviet involvement in Afghanistan.

Such moves may have helped bring Iraq and South Yemen back into the mainstream of Gulf acceptability during the 1980s. Riyadh's purchase of the Chinese missiles may have been intended, at least in part, to demonstrate independence of action *vis-à-vis* the US. Although careful not to break Arab ranks on Israel, Riyadh has hosted delegations of prominent American Jews in efforts to explain its position on Arab–Israeli matters and to defuse criticism of its domestic affairs.

Financial assistance

Monetary inducements can persuade but they are not very reliable deterrents (the payment of millions of dollars in war loans to Iraq during the 1980s did not protect either Kuwait or Saudi Arabia in 1990). Since the beginning of its oil era, and especially since the oil price revolution of 1973–74, Saudi Arabia has embarked on a multi-faceted programme of aid and disbursement. Between 1975 and 1987 the $48bn the Kingdom gave to developing countries (second only to the United States' aid contributions) averaged 4.2% of its GNP.[33]

In part, financial assistance has been routinised and channelled through established institutions, some of them multilateral bodies, such as the World Bank and the UN Development Organisation. The Saudi government has also worked through regional institutions, notably the Islamic Development Bank, the Arab Fund for Economic and Social Development, the OPEC Fund for International Development and the Organisation of the Islamic Conference. Bilateral financial relationships have been conducted on an *ad hoc* basis, through programmes administered by the Saudi Development Fund and by initiating regular programmes of payments, such as the already mentioned subventions to the Palestine Liberation Organisation and subsequently the Palestinian Authority.

The Islamic dimension

Saudi Arabia sees itself as having special responsibilities in the worldwide Islamic community. This attitude derives from two sources. The first is the eighteenth-century alliance between the Al Saud and religious reformer Muhammad Abd al-Wahhab, and the historic perception of the Al Saud that they have a special role to play as the agents of Islamic purification. This Islamic element in the legitimacy of the Al Saud leads the Kingdom to proclaim itself as the quintessential Islamic state. For this reason, the country exhibits an extraordinary religious and social conservatism, as a result of which the government finds it extremely difficult to make many domestic changes.

The second Islamic responsibility comes from Saudi control of the two holiest cities in Islam: Mecca, with the great mosque housing the *Ka'bah* (the small building that forms the spiritual and geographic centre of Islam), and Medina, the burial place of the Prophet Muhammad. The international responsibilities devolving on the Saudi state include both the administration of the *haj* (the annual pilgrimage to Mecca of Muslims from all over the world) and a role as spokesman and advocate for Islamic causes throughout the world.

In practical terms, Saudi Arabia sponsors an Islamic foreign policy that operates alongside its secular foreign policy. The two may link up on certain issues: for example, support for beleaguered Muslim populations in countries such as Afghanistan and Bosnia. Another congruence lies in Saudi Arabia's founding of, and its strong support for, such entities as the World Muslim League and the Organisation of the Islamic Conference (OIC), which help to enhance Saudi Arabia's aura of leadership throughout the Islamic world.[34]

Over the course of the twentieth century, the Saudi regime has established a formidable array of religious and quasi-religious organs intended to promote Islam within and outside the country. Over time, many of these organs acquired an independence based on the reluctance of secular authorities to interfere with their unimpeachable religious duty. Thus in many respects the Islamic foreign policy operates independently of the Foreign Ministry. Various components engage in proselytisation, the construction of mosques in Islamic countries and the distribution of Korans around the world. The constituents of the Islamic foreign policy may even cut across the secular foreign policy: in countries of mixed religion, such as Sudan or Nigeria, the Islamic foreign-policy objective of propagating Islam may undermine the secular policy aim of maintaining good relations with the governments. This became a matter of particular concern after the 11 September attacks.

The Kingdom therefore faces a dilemma not unlike the one faced by the new Soviet Union when it was forced to choose between serving as the vanguard of an international revolutionary movement and accepting the responsibilities of a nation-state in an international community. Whilst Saudi Arabia's secular foreign policy seeks to ensure the physical security of the country via whatever means and alliances apply, the Islamic foreign policy is engaged in promoting a religious agenda of a particularly conservative nature. The problem is made more complex when the Islamic foreign policy interacts with devout private citizens in the context of humanitarian aid and religious support. Inevitably some use the mantle of religion for political purposes. The provision of official and unofficial Saudi support for Muslims fighting the Soviet forces in Afghanistan led to the phenomenon of the 'Arab Afghans', one of whom was Osama bin Laden. Thus, reactionary Muslim elements solicit and receive financial assistance that is distributed to radical groups around the world, such as the Chechen resistance in Russia, Kashmiri separatists in India and the Abu Sayyaf guerrillas in the Philippines.

Old themes, new emphases

Saudi foreign policy has been remarkably constant over the last few decades, and there is little need to change – indeed little room for manoeuvre. The Saudis remain heavily committed to their partnership with the United States, and it would be counterproductive for either Riyadh or Washington to alter relations. The Kingdom also values its economic, political and security relations with other Western countries. Saudi Arabia continues to carry considerable weight in Arab circles, and this factor – along with genuine concern over the plight of the Palestinians and an attempt to dampen the most troubling source of Saudi–American friction – undoubtedly lay behind Prince Abdullah's initiative for Arab–Israeli peace in February 2002.

Saudi Arabia's cardinal concern remains the Gulf, of course. Its fraternal relations with other GCC members continue to be strong, but Riyadh has also worked assiduously to improve relations with Iran, and the Bush administration's adoption of a hard-line *vis-à-vis* the Islamic Republic adds another complication to US–Saudi relations. Iraq, however, remains the second most troubling point of friction between Riyadh and Washington. Iraq is still beyond the pale, but there is some feeling in the Kingdom that re-integrating it into the Arab system is not incompatible with the desired removal of Saddam Hussein. The Bush administration's growing bellicosity on Iraq undoubtedly causes sleepless nights in Riyadh.

It may still be too early to gauge the impact of September 2001 on the Islamic dimension of Saudi foreign policy, but it is clear that Saudi Arabia has been embarrassed by its handling of the Taliban and Osama bin Laden, as well as by criticism of Wahabism and 'Wahabi' proselytising outside the Kingdom. It has already placed well-publicised restrictions on Islamic charities sending funds abroad, and it is quite likely that there will be stricter central government supervision of other Islamic propagation activities. Beyond Afghanistan, South Asia continues to be troublesome for Saudi foreign policy. Riyadh has no choice but to support Pakistan, just as the United States discovered for itself after 11 September, but it remains troubled by that state's continuing weakness, sectarian strife and the refuge provided to al-Qaeda in ungoverned areas. In addition, there remains the real threat of war between Pakistan and India and the collateral damage that would cause in the Gulf.

Saudi Arabia and the West: divergent security expectations?

Reliance on the United States as a partner in and guarantor of Saudi security has become the central pillar of Saudi strategy. The Kingdom has based its security needs, and therefore its alliance with America, on the dependability and credibility of the US strategic 'umbrella'. This does not mean, of course, that Washington and Riyadh see eye-to-eye on all means of providing that security, let alone on all the issues involved.

Since the collapse of the Soviet Union, Western policy has centred the maintenance of Gulf security on containing Iraq and Iran. The West requires Saudi Arabia, as well as the other the GCC members, to participate in this strategy, because measures taken in the name of Gulf security are taken ostensibly to defend GCC states, either through territorial protection (e.g. preventing an Iraqi invasion of Kuwait or Saudi Arabia) or by protecting oil (its production and transport out of the Gulf – and hence continuing revenues for the GCC states).

GCC cooperation is needed to enforce the policy of containment: GCC states provide facilities for *Southern Watch*, the programme for enforcing the 'no-fly' zone in Iraq's largely Shiite south, and permit the use of their ports for Western naval visits and refuelling. At the same time, the West needs the political backing of Saudi Arabia and the GCC for its political goals and arrangements in order to maintain the legitimacy of the policy.

A foundation of the relationship between the West and Saudi Arabia is that a tacit *quid pro quo* exists. Saudi Arabia will seek to provide sufficient oil at reasonable prices and will recycle its income by purchasing arms and other Western goods; in return the West will provide protection from external threats and favourable trading terms and will invest in Saudi Arabia through offset programmes.[35] By this conception, the relationship between the West and the Kingdom should involve rapport on various planes, including military cooperation, political and diplomatic congruence and an integrated security framework.

A fundamental principle of the Western conception is that a direct and continuing US and Western military presence in the Gulf region is required. The most permanent element of this presence is the US Navy's Fifth Fleet, which has operated out of Bahrain since the 1940s. For most of this period its major mission has been to fly the flag, since its operational capability was always too small to constitute a deterrent by itself. Since the 1987 'tanker war', though, the US Navy has maintained a more robust presence in the region by rotating task forces, including carrier groups, through the Gulf and surrounding waters. European nations have contributed smaller flotillas from time to time, and regular naval visits have become routine. Another aspect of the American and British (and initially French) presence has been the operation of personnel and equipment to sustain *Southern Watch*. More substantial Western military presence in the Gulf has come through bilateral relationships with Gulf allies. For several decades, these relationships have included negotiated agreements for access to local facilities and the prepositioning of supplies for emergency use. Facility access primarily has meant use of air installations, including Prince Sultan Air Base at al-Kharj in Saudi Arabia.

Another important aspect of the military relationship is the supply of arms, equipment, materiel, training and other support to Gulf allies. Saudi Arabia has been amongst the world's largest arms purchasers over the last several decades, and the lion's share of the transactions has involved Western countries. The scale of some of these deals is enormous and involves many complications; a good example is the two *al-Yamamah* deals between Britain and Saudi Arabia. In the mid-1980s the Kingdom encountered difficulties getting US Congressional approval of arms sales agreed with the American administration, and so turned to Britain. The result was the *al-Yamamah-I* arms deal of 1985, with a total value of some $5–7bn, for 72 *Tornado* combat aircraft and 60 other aircraft. The cost was to be financed by oil deliveries to Britain and, in an 'offset' deal, Britain undertook to invest some of its proceeds in Saudi industrialisation projects. But three years later all this was dwarfed by *al-Yamamah-II*, a truly massive arms deal worth between $12bn and $25bn and including 50 more *Tornados*, 60 *Hawk* trainer aircraft, 50 *Blackhawk* helicopters, six minesweepers and the building of several large air bases. The subsequent decline in oil prices, however, meant that substantial parts of the order were cancelled or delayed in following years.

Just as important as arms sales are military training programmes. These range from long-term training and professional-isation support for entire services (such as the American programme for the modernisation of the Saudi National Guard) to the short-term provision of training on newly acquired arms. In addition to in-country assistance, all Western countries provide places in staff colleges and other military educational establishments for Saudi officers. The value of these programmes goes far beyond the specific training involved to the creation of life-long bonds of camaraderie and cooperation. Another means of strengthening military ties is through official visits (notably by the Commander-in-Chief and staff of the US Central Command) and joint exercises with some GCC states.

Equally important for Western goals is the maintenance of a common political front. Washington has regularly pressured Saudi Arabia to back the US position on Iraqi sanctions and the no-fly zones, which, officially and formally, Riyadh has done with varying degrees of reluctance. Inducing Riyadh to provide diplomatic support for the Western policy of containing Iran has been more difficult, for Saudi Arabia has pursued a policy of rapprochement with the Islamic Republic in recent years, despite Washington's misgivings and intimations that Iran was behind the barracks bombing in al-Khobar.[36]

More generally, the West seeks to encourage the Gulf states to exercise moderation on other Arab states *vis-à-vis* Israel (which included persuading Oman and Qatar to permit Israeli trade missions in their capitals) and to exert their influence on unfriendly Arab states such as Syria and Libya. Beyond this, the West desires a coordination of interests and relations between the Gulf states and other American allies in the region, such as Egypt, Jordan and Turkey, in order to build up a coalition of partners against common enemies. Finally, of course, the West expects Saudi Arabia to exercise its influence in OPEC councils in favour of abundant oil supplies and against actions that will raise prices. Furthermore, the West wants Saudi Arabia to persuade the GCC as a whole to adopt pro-Western policies, even though – or perhaps because – the security relationship between the West and the GCC itself has been seriously under-developed, probably because it has been easier for Western policy-makers to deal with individual governments than with the GCC as a single entity.

Despite Western efforts to cajole Saudi Arabia to follow its lead, a fundamental question remains unanswered. To what extent are Western conceptions of Gulf security predicated on real Saudi needs, and especially on requirements that do not dovetail with Western interests?

Just as Saudi Arabia is the cornerstone of Western strategic policy, the United States – and, to a lesser extent, other European powers – has been the cornerstone of Saudi strategic policy. The principal Saudi relationship is with the United States, and military ties are entwined in many ways. Recent defence expenditures for Saudi Arabia alone have averaged around $20bn a year, and the Kingdom received arms deliveries worth $65.9bn between 1993 and 2000.[37] Over the years the United States has been the principal supplier of arms to the Kingdom, and the bulk of air force and army equipment is purchased from the US. The total value of arms agreements from 1950 to early 1997 was $93.8bn. Agreements from 1991 to 1998 totalled $22.8bn in value, about 20% of which was for lethal equipment, more than 30% for support services, and somewhat less than 20% for building military bases and facilities (mostly completed before 1990).[38] The US Army Corps of Engineers long played a prominent role in Saudi development projects and was responsible for the construction of a number of Saudi military facilities. The principal element of US military assistance at present is the US training mission to the Saudi Arabian National Guard, involving nearly 100 US personnel.[39] In addition, private defence contractors continue to provide many services.

Although the United States is by far Saudi Arabia's most important military supplier, the Saudis have been careful to share out their purchases. Thus Britain won the two *al-Yamamah* contracts mentioned earlier, and the French play a leading role in supplying and advising the navy. Of the $65.9bn of arms deliveries received by the Kingdom during 1993–2000, Britain, France, Germany and Italy provided $31.5bn, compared to $28.3bn from the United States.[40] Extending the use of military facilities for regional operations (such as *Southern Watch*) and providing in-country assistance have been other means of assuring assistance when required as well.

But heavy reliance on the United States carries many risks. When the dominant partner in a big power/small power relationship is also the world's sole superpower, the small power must be prepared to have its arm twisted. This has been apparent, for example, in pressure to buy American goods, pressure to buy American arms, pressure to provide greater access to local military facilities and insistence on some degree of extra-territoriality for American service personnel. In addition, the penalty of close identification with the United States is that this often attracts criticism, both domestically and from abroad, because of American policies elsewhere in the region and world. Moreover, close connections with Israel's strongest supporter are viewed with dismay by many sectors of Saudi Arabia's population and provoke strong denunciations from other countries. (Of course, this also means that US policy objectives *vis-à-vis* Saudi Arabia and the Gulf, especially arms sales, are vulnerable to pressure and disruption by Israel and its supporters in the US.) Underlying everything, though, is a fear – rarely voiced officially but frequently discussed privately – that Washington may not be a reliable ally. After all, the somewhat paradoxical arguments go, the US walked away when the Shah's regime began to crumble, and strong declarations of commitment in places like Lebanon and Somalia quickly disappeared when American soldiers died.

The present security arrangements have evolved over the course of decades and undoubtedly are the most efficient possible under current Gulf security conceptions. It is highly unlikely that either the will or the capacity exists for a Western security umbrella without the US. Japan already imports a large amount of Gulf oil, and China and even India are likely to greatly increase their imports in the next decade, yet Japan's ability to contribute to Gulf security is minimal, and there is little likelihood of either China or India doing any more.

Political considerations would seem to doom any significant long-term provision of Arab forces. The promise of the Damascus Declaration, tying the GCC with Syria and Egypt, the two most prominent Arab participants in Operation *Desert Storm*, quickly evaporated and has become a dead issue. There remains the question of what effective role collective security within the GCC might play.

The regional framework: GCC collective security

Saudi security concerns have been inextricably linked to those of its five allies in the GCC since the formation of the alliance in 1981. The GCC states share common threat perceptions and military limitations, and they have pursued similar defensive strategies and sought collaborative defence arrangements. Thus it makes sense to discuss Saudi and GCC concerns together. The fundamental defence policy on which the Gulf states have relied since the formation of the GCC (and before) has been a holding strategy of initial self-defence until the Western cavalry arrives from over the horizon. Gulf governments have sought to guarantee this protection for themselves by several means.

One method is to sign direct bilateral agreements: in the years after its liberation, Kuwait negotiated bilateral agreements with the US, Britain and France. Bilateral military exercises also strengthen at least the aura of cooperation. Another technique is to buy arms and other military equipment from protecting countries. The Gulf states have consistently ranked among the top arms purchasers in the world. In 1997 Saudi Arabia ranked ninth in the world in military expenditures ($21.195bn), even though the size of its armed forces (180,000) ranked thirty-first. It was also the world's largest arms importer ($11.6bn), and the other GCC members ranked fifth (Kuwait, $2bn), ninth (UAE, $1.4bn), eighteenth (Qatar, $625m), forty-fifth (Oman, $160m) and fifty-ninth (Bahrain, $90m).[41] Gulf countries often pay top price for such arms and equipment, and frequently also buy an entire package of supplies and training, which adds considerably to the transaction cost. Furthermore, since many such purchases are top-of-the-line, the deal with Gulf buyers extends the production run and reduces the unit cost, which benefits the armed forces of the protecting powers as well. Gulf states typically over-buy for their current needs, thus possibly providing a store of arms and supplies that could be used by allies in an emergency.

In many ways, the six GCC members are perfectly matched: they are all monarchies with tribally based ruling families, and they have small, relatively homogenous societies and oil-dependent economies. Yet there are two principal factors that inhibit cooperation and coordination of policies in all spheres, including security strategy. The first is that, although Saudi Arabia may be a small state on the world stage, it is a giant in comparison to its GCC partners (or, as one prominent Saudi put it in a private conversation, the GCC consists of a shark and five little fish). Among other things, this inequality reduces the prospects for further GCC integration, because further steps in this direction inevitably will increase Saudi domination of the alliance and control over its neighbours. This would appear to be the principal obstacle, for example, behind the failure of the GCC to implement the proposal made by Sultan Qabus of Oman after the liberation of Kuwait to expand the small joint Peninsula Shield Force to 100,000 men.[42]

The second problem appears on closer examination of the GCC states. While they are similar and compatible in many respects, there is among the six countries a historical pattern of hostility between immediate neighbours, and the smaller countries (with the exception of Bahrain) have all experienced Saudi aggression over the past two centuries. This means that relations within the GCC can be prickly, and even severely strained. Until recently Bahrain and Qatar have been at loggerheads over a number of territorial questions; Saudi–Qatari relations flare up at intervals over seemingly trivial matters; and it took until the late 1990s for Oman and the UAE to establish embassies in each other's capitals.

Still, the GCC members have little choice but to stick together. To extend the piscine metaphor above, the GCC states can be characterised as small fish in a glass bowl with cats for neighbours. The requirement for coordinated security strategy is obvious and recognised, but achieving the necessary coordination has been an uphill struggle. Even well after the Iranian Revolution and the eruption of the Iran–Iraq War, Kuwait continued to insist that Gulf security was a purely regional affair, and that the great powers should keep their distance. Oman was seen within the alliance as the odd man out for its insistence that security depended on close and dependable military relationships with Western countries.

Kuwaiti attitudes flip-flopped with the tanker war in 1987, and then rapidly moved to the other extreme after the Iraqi invasion in 1990, but serious disagreements persist. GCC military committees and summits issue statements of impending cooperation in air defence; the token Peninsula Shield Force exists; and bilateral and joint exercises are held regularly. Yet the states all pursue independent and uncoordinated procurement policies; they buy from an enormous range of suppliers; the exercises are staged largely for show; and the Peninsula Shield Force is chiefly symbolic.

Disagreements continue to include differences over how far cooperation with the United States and the West is desirable. For example, Oman and Qatar are criticised for having allowed Israel to open trade offices, presumably at the insistence of the US. The rift is seen internally as well, with the Kuwaiti National Assembly opposing the ruling family's perceived acquiescence in US demands, and with the existence of some organised clandestine opposition to the US presence in Saudi Arabia. While such quarrels are not likely to split the alliance (just as rows within ruling families are firmly kept in house), a fissiparous potential does exist, as exemplified a few years ago, when Qatar's new ruler seemed to emphasise ties to Iran and the United States as a counter to perceived GCC betrayal.

From the Saudi point of view, continued close cooperation with the GCC is necessary. The smaller Gulf states constitute Riyadh's vulnerable underbelly, and their defence is vital to the defence of the Kingdom itself. It stands to reason that closer co-ordination in security matters – whether it be expanded joint forces, a GCC-wide early-warning system, or reciprocal agreements that an attack upon one member is an attack upon all – will improve the security prospects of Saudi Arabia as much as or more than those of the GCC as a whole. In addition, even closer GCC integration is probably desirable for the Saudis, largely for the reasons that give the other Gulf states pause: the Kingdom's overwhelming relative size would mean greater Saudi authority in GCC political and security discussions, as well as economies of scale in an expanded economic market.

In short, Saudi Arabia's security depends on close and mutually beneficial relations with both the United States and the GCC, and, to a lesser extent, with other Western powers and Arab friends. Protection against the potentially threatening remainder of the world necessarily depends in the first instance on Saudi and GCC self-defence and ultimately on the Western strategic umbrella. There is no viable alternative on the current horizon. Paradoxically, though, strengthening ties to both the US and the GCC creates new problems and/or exacerbates existing ones. While the relationship with the GCC is not likely to change substantially in the next decade or two, the Saudi–American connection will be tested by a number of issues, such as Israel and Palestine, policy towards Iraq, bilateral cooperation in the light of 11 September, American actions *vis-à-vis* the Arab and Islamic worlds and developments inside Saudi Arabia.

Chapter 2

The internal dimensions of Saudi security

Successful security for the GCC and the Gulf depends in no small measure on domestic developments in Saudi Arabia and its GCC allies. Prominent among these is the question of succession, both as regards the specific heirs to the present rulers and, more fundamentally, in terms of future directions of succession within ruling families and the new roles to be played by changing societies.[1] Saudi Arabia is nearing completion of the first phase of socio-economic development – building a physical and social infrastructure – and faces the more formidable challenge of a creating self-sustaining economy. Despite outward appearances and government protestations, this engenders significant social change that is likely to lead to demands for fuller participation in decision-making – with obvious ramifications for current policies that rely heavily on personal relations between Western governments and the Al Saud ruling family.

Saudi citizens are becoming increasingly sceptical that Gulf security depends on an alliance with the West that has as its principal objective the containment of Iraq and Iran. Whereas the regime has seen its interests, both in foreign-policy considerations and in regime survival, bound to the establishment and maintenance of close alliance with the West (primarily the US and Britain), many in the Kingdom, at all levels of society, express growing mistrust of the United States, its actions and its policies.

They object to close ties with the United States because of two American policies that have a strong negative impact in the region.

First, they see American actions towards Iraq, backed by Britain, as being primarily responsible for creating the present humanitarian plight of the Iraqi people, and they do not perceive continued sanctions as being useful. Second, they have become increasingly angered by what they regard as Israeli oppression of the Palestinians and by what seems to them to be overwhelmingly uncritical American support of Israel. (Particularly since the second *intifada* began in October 2000, several Gulf regimes have suffered widespread criticism from their people for these alliances). There are many in Saudi Arabia who also believe that the United States and the West exaggerate the dangers from Iraq and Iran in order to sell arms to the Gulf states at inflated prices. Some even believe that they are deliberately prolonging Iraq's international quarantine in order to sell more arms and keep the Gulf states dependent on the West.

The American war on Osama bin Laden and the Taliban regime in Afghanistan has raised fresh suspicions among many Saudis that the United States is fundamentally hostile to Islam. Notwithstanding their widespread opposition to American policy *vis-à-vis* Israel, this is unlikely to be the view of many middle-class Saudis; on the other hand, many lesser-educated and untravelled Saudis may hold this belief, however viscerally.[2]

The impact of economic and social change in Saudi Arabia inevitably will cause political repercussions, including re-examination of the role of the ruling families and pressure for political participation. Just as inevitably the evolution away from what some have called a 'rentier' society will redefine the basis of the 'social compact' between rulers and ruled and direct more emphasis towards issues that Saudi citizens – as well as the regime – consider important. These concerns lie at the heart of the internal dimension of Saudi security. A brief look at changes occurring in Saudi society will illustrate the background to many of these attitudes and issues.

Changing society

Saudi society has evolved tremendously during the past 30 or more years, and the impact of economic change and progress in development has been to transform many traditional social relationships and to create new expectations and demands. This process has been accentuated by shifts in social class and demography.

The impact of economic change and development

Since the 1960s the Kingdom has embarked on a colossal programme of economic development, particularly through a series of ambitious five-year plans. The first plan (1970–75), overtaken by the explosion of oil prices during 1973–4, was followed by a much better-endowed and more ambitious second plan (1975–80) that emphasised infrastructure improvements, heavy defence expenditures and the immense industrialisation projects at the new cities of Jubayl (on the Gulf) and Yanbu (on the Red Sea). Increasing domestic production, especially in agriculture, and greater emphasis on the role of the private sector were the focus of the next four five-year plans, with an added effort since 2000 to reduce dependence on oil revenues and to develop human resources, implement privatisation policy and improve productivity within the government.

The social impact of this process of development has been enormous, despite the traditionally conservative nature of Saudi society and the government's conscious efforts to foster economic change while simultaneously seeking to avoid social change. Not surprisingly, rising standards of living and better health care have resulted in a population explosion. An annual population growth rate estimated at 4.5% in 1990 and 2.6% in 1999 has resulted in a total population officially estimated at 21.3m – including 5.7m expatriates (as of 1999) – and projected to rise to 33.7m by 2015.[3] Some 50% of this population is under 18,[4] and the education pipeline is full from end to end. The result is more than 175,000 new secondary-school graduates each year, most of whom are now having great difficulty in finding employment. Dissatisfaction and despair today can easily turn to bitterness and alienation tomorrow.

Another important change has been the urbanisation of the population. The urban proportion of the Kingdom's population stood at 85% of the total in 1999.[5] Riyadh's population, estimated at 30,000 in 1930 and 300,000 in 1968, stood at 1.2m in the 1974 census and is presently estimated at 3.5m.[6] Jeddah and the Eastern Province conurbation of Dhahran, Dammam and al-Khobar are not far behind. Such demographic shifts have grave implications for tribal and regional loyalties or identities, for relationships within extended families and for the manner in which peer groups are formed. Increasingly, personal connections are being made in ways similar to the West, rather than by traditional ties of family and tribal relationships.[7]

At the same time, there have been wide-ranging shifts in occupation, as much of the population has moved from traditional pastoral, agricultural and fishing lifestyles to government employment or to employment in the modern private sector. Education has created a bulge of mid-level government employees, public- and private-sector managers, military officers, educators and small business entrepreneurs. The consequence is the rise of a substantial middle class (or as some Saudis term it, 'middle-income class') that display many of the same values and goals as middle-class counterparts around the world: greater emphasis on the nuclear family, the building of private villa-style residences, career advancement in salaried positions and so forth.[8]

Perhaps the greatest impact has been in the field of education. The total of enrolled students in all educational institutions rose from 547,000 in 1969/1970 to nearly five million in 1998/1999. The numbers of intermediate and secondary school students rose from 77,000 to 1.8m in the same period, while university students increased from 7,000 to 343,000.[9] Considerable emphasis has been placed on higher education, concentrating initially on education overseas but subsequently on the development of indigenous universities. One effect of this growing redirection of government scholarship students at university and postgraduate levels is the loss of personal experience of the West and reduced familiarity with Western life, values and ways. The less Saudi students are exposed to direct contact with the United States or Europe, the more they will tend to accept negative stereotypes and political animosity. In the 1970s and 1980s more than 30,000 Saudi students studied in the United States each year; now there are less than 6,000.[10] Most Saudi students and children of any age do not have – and are unlikely to have – any direct contact with the United States (the heavily publicised detention of Saudi students in the United States after 11 September has only worsened this trend).

Another effect of the expansion of Saudi education has to do with the distinction between 'secular' and 'Islamic' universities. The former are modelled on Western institutions; the latter were created originally to provide instruction for *ulama* (religious scholars), *qadis* (judges), *imams* (prayer leaders) and other religious functionaries. Over the years, the Islamic universities have tended to attract a number of less-qualified students and are generally regarded as having lower academic standards. Not surprisingly, they are centres of conservative Islamic sentiment, including anti-Western and anti-regime feeling. It has long been alleged that, as academically poor students drop out of secular universities, they are able continue their studies in Islamic universities, and at least some of them are then influenced by the reactionary elements.[11]

Not surprisingly, religious feelings and institutions have been strongly affected by social change. Saudi Arabia takes pride in describing itself as an 'Islamic state' whose affairs are governed by the *sharia* (Islamic law). The central role and influence of the religious establishment in the Saudi state has long been a major constraint on the latitude of government action; the government must often strike a compromise with the *ulama* in order to get their approval for the introduction of innovations. But the emergence of more radical, anti-government and non-government-approved Islamists introduces another layer of Islam-based conservative complications into the government's calculations. Ever since the siege of the Great Mosque of Mecca in 1979 by disaffected young, anti-establishment Islamists or neo-Ikhwan,[12] there has been a tension between the officially appointed and approved religious establishment and (often younger) anti-government religious critics.

At the same time, Saudi society is influenced by external factors. Satellite television has permitted information and opinions to be absorbed from sources other than government-controlled media, and the emergence of Arabic-language channels such as the Middle East Broadcasting Corporation and especially the iconoclastic Jazeera Television of Qatar has resulted in an audience that extends well beyond the Western-educated elites. It should be remembered, too, that religious viewpoints may be spread by such media just as easily as political ones, and the role of audio cassettes in disseminating divergent and subversive opinions is well known throughout the Middle East.

Saudi Arabia's successful entry into the World Trade Organisation will also entail fundamental changes. The reduction and elimination of subsidies to Saudi industry has already improved the prospects for tighter economic integration within the GCC. With WTO membership, the Saudi economy will undergo significant liberalisation; businesses will find themselves facing foreign competition at home and the government will be required to adopt more transparency and reform in its economic structure. The privileged role of the ruling family in the economic sphere will undoubtedly be challenged. The privatisation of Saudi Arabian Airlines provides a pertinent example of the changes required: the sale of the airline depends on its being made profitable, and profitability means that the ruling family members' privilege of pre-empting other passengers and flying for free must end. This has direct political implications for the ruling caste's monopoly of power.

The political framework and emerging strains

Not unexpectedly, the process of rapid economic and social change has serious political ramifications, despite official assertions to the contrary. Although the Kingdom has built a modern government and bureaucracy, the fact remains that the Al Saud royal family dominate the country in nearly all spheres. On the one hand, the Al Saud hold the country together and provide the stability that has produced relative prosperity for nearly all Saudi citizens. On the other hand, the concentration of power and privilege in the hands of a single caste imposes a tremendous burden on the country and engenders widespread resentment. Yet, while voices of dissent multiply, the regime's response to the issue of political participation is widely seen as too little and too ineffective.

Old elites and new elites

Change has produced a mix of old and new elites. Some of the old elites have successfully expanded their power; others have seen their standing diminish, sometimes quite severely. New elites, by definition, are newcomers in terms of power relationships, and consequently their power and influence are necessarily limited.

The most important elite in the country is, of course, the Al Saud. Although membership is determined by heredity, thus effectively making it a caste, the family is of considerable size and expanding – the number of male members is not known, but estimates range up to 10,000. The King stands at the apex of this family hierarchy, along with his brothers and other close relations, and they form an inner decision-making elite. A second level consists of the descendants of King Abd al-Aziz (ruled 1902–53), which includes not only the king and his full and half-brothers, but also the grandsons and great-grandsons of Abd al-Aziz. At the outer edges are the cadet branches – Al Saud al-Kabir, Al Farhan, Al Thunayan, Al Turki and Al Jiluwi, which have lost many family privileges but still rank above the commoners.

Most of the other old elites are diminishing in importance. The Al al-Sheikh, descendants of Muhammad 'Abd al-Wahhab, have long played an important secondary role as the religious guardians of the state and society. Until recently, it looked as if their influence was waning, particularly as non-family members took over many of the top religious positions. This seemed in part to be a consequence of the natural expansion of other candidates into these positions, though there may well also have been a deliberate effort by the Al Saud to dilute the power of the Al al-Sheikh. However, as of 2002, members of the Al al-Sheikh were serving as ministers of Islamic Guidance, Justice, and State, and President of the Higher Council of Ulama. The status and influence of the *ulama* and other religious functionaries has also seemed to diminish – mostly because of growing social complexity and their reduction to salaried government servants, but also because of the rise of hostile Islamic forces and ideologies.

The importance of the tribal sheikhs, at least on the national scene, has also seemed to be waning. In part this was a natural evolution as the centre of gravity of the state's defences and coercive power shifted from the support of loyal tribal levies to more organised institutions such as the armed forces, National Guard and police units. In addition, urbanisation and competition from new elites increasingly restricted the sheikhs' influence to internal tribal matters. In years past, alienating the tribal sheikhs could well lead to serious repercussions; with the development of a more complex state structure and security organs, though, it is unlikely that any tribally based dissidence would get very far now. This does not, of course, rule out tribal rivalries within the Army or National Guard, for example, or a belief that one tribe receives more favoured treatment than another – but such developments are not likely to turn actively hostile.

The burden and resilience of the Al Saud

There are more than a few Saudis who feel that the royal family is a burden on the state. As the family effectively controls the receipt and distribution of oil income on behalf of the state, the opportunities for family members to abuse a national trust are virtually unlimited. Additional royal privileges, such as access to government positions, free air travel and so forth, fill ordinary Saudis with resentment. On the other hand, the Al Saud perform at least two vital functions. First, they are the glue that holds the country together. The present Kingdom has been created out of a hodgepodge of Arabia's regions: the Eastern Province, holding nearly all the country's oil and looking to the Gulf for identity; the Hijaz in the west, home to Islam's holiest places, with a population of heterogeneous origins and an independent Kingdom until the 1920s; the populous south, geographically and culturally close to Yemen; the lightly populated deserts of the north, with great nomadic tribes that spill over into Jordan, Syria and Iraq; and the central region of Najd, home of the Al Saud and the most conservative part of the Kingdom. At various times in the last two centuries the Al Saud have conquered these disparate regions, and since the 1930s (when the name 'Kingdom of Saudi Arabia' was adopted) have absorbed them permanently. Without the unifying and controlling force of the royal family, there seems little reason for these regions to hang together.

On a more personal level, the Al Saud provide the most senior members of the government – King, Heir Apparent, Prime Minister and Deputy Prime Ministers, and the ministers of Defence and Aviation, Interior, Foreign Affairs, Public Works and Housing, and a Minister of State. Younger members of the family are liberally scattered throughout key ministries, the armed forces and the oil industry. While many family members have neither the aptitude nor the discipline necessary to occupy important positions, it is surprising how many others are well-suited to government work.

The issue of political participation

In common with its Gulf allies, Saudi Arabia faces growing pressures for political participation, at least from the expanding educated sector of its population. The shape of participation perceived to be required may not conform to Western models, such as parliamentary democracy, and its scope may well not extend as far as a process of direct elections. Nonetheless, it is clear that a growing desire is emerging for a say in state and government objectives, for fora in which to debate national issues, for the creation of some form of government accountability, and for restrictions on the role and excesses of members of ruling families.

The principal response of the Saudi government to date has been the creation of the *Majlis al-Shura*, or Consultative Council, in

1993. Vague plans and promises for a consultative council of some sort had been floated in Riyadh since the time of King Faisal, and King Fahd reiterated his intention to establish a council on various occasions throughout the 1980s – premises were even built for it adjacent to the new King's Office Complex in Riyadh.[13] In 1992 the announcement was finally made that an appointed *Majlis al-Shura* would be established, and over the following months a former Minister of Justice was named as Chairman, 60 members were appointed, and the new *majlis* held its first session in December 1993. The second *majlis* (1997–2001) saw its membership increased to 90 members, and the third *majlis* (2001–2005) saw another increase to 120 members. Increasingly the emphasis seemed to be on younger modernists with higher degrees.[14] The *majlis* is not a legislative body, and its purview is limited to the social-service functions of government. Nonetheless, it is said to discuss vigorously a variety of issues in committee; several ministers have briefed the council on developments in their fields; and a growing number of young ministers have been drawn from the council's ranks.

It is highly unlikely, however, that any direct form of elections will transpire in the foreseeable future, nor is the government likely to liberalise domestic media or professional organisations. Still, pressure undoubtedly will grow in coming years, as Saudis witness developments around them in the Gulf.

Defence issues and the social compact

Needless to say, internal changes have direct implications for Saudi defence and security policy. This may take several forms. The long decline in oil revenues (only recently, and perhaps temporarily, reversed) has produced the equivalent of a 'guns or butter' debate; this is almost inseparable from widespread perceptions that many, or most, defence expenditures occur simply as a means to enrich members of the ruling family and their cronies. The regime's heavy reliance on the 'special relationship' with the United States forms another area of disagreement. And furthermore, insofar as Saudi Arabia can be regarded as a rentier state, how far is it reasonable to expect its citizenry to feel a sense of commitment and obligation towards national defence? Differences over defence and security concerns may well prove to be the weakest aspect of the Saudi 'social compact'.

'Guns or butter'

As we have seen, the Kingdom of Saudi Arabia has been one of the world's biggest arms-purchasing states. The pattern of heavy purchases began after the oil–price revolution and continued through the 1980s. Major acquisitions since the Kuwait War have included more than 700 tanks, several hundred armoured personnel carriers, nearly 1,000 light armoured vehicles, several frigates, 72 additional F-15 combat aircraft and several dozen *Patriot* missile batteries.[15] In the later 1990s, however, falling oil prices resulted in a drastic cutback in arms purchases[16] – even as Saudi Arabia's leaders perceived increased security needs, budget problems curtailed their expenditures. Between 1984/5 and 1999, government spending outran revenues by an average of $13bn a year,[17] creating the need to make difficult choices between competing claims on the government purse. From an economic point of view, the logical step would be to reduce consumer and other subsidies, and indeed the government did act to reduce high subsidies to wheat farmers. But the government has been loath to increase living costs at a time when average per capita income has been falling and prospects for many young Saudis are dim. Some effort was made to increase electricity charges, and petrol prices were raised in 1999. But the government has preferred generally to delay payments, issue bonds and even borrow on the international market rather than risk a public backlash on utility prices.

Complaints about military expenditures are increasingly heard in private conversation across a wide spectrum of the population. Such complaints adopt several forms. One is the straight 'guns or butter' argument, pointing out that the purchase of arms and other materiel reduces the money available for social services or development programmes. In addition, with the shrinking of the economic pie, the issue of corruption has risen to the surface. Paying public officials commissions on military and other state purchases, for example, is not *per se* illegal in the Kingdom, and so does not technically constitute corruption. Nevertheless, popular opinion increasingly regards such commissions – along with such practices as selling dubiously acquired land to the government at inflated practices and the rigged awarding of contracts to members of the ruling family and allied elites – as symptomatic of a corrupt system, particularly objectionable at a time when the average standard of living has fallen so significantly. In particular, the role in these practices of the Al Saud, who already receive direct stipends from oil revenues, is seen as unfair advantage. Arms deals are regarded as the biggest source of corruption, and some argue that fattening pockets is just as big a factor in such deals as legitimate national needs. Others turn the argument slightly and ask why it is necessary to pay for arms when Saudi Arabia also has to pay for Western states to defend it.

Citizenry defence participation in a rentier state

Two concepts seem to underlie a negative view of universal citizen participation in defence issues in the Kingdom. The first is that, in the absence of taxation, means of government accountability and public participation in formulating a national defence framework (as well as discussing the specific issues around which defence is required), there seems to be little reason for many citizens to feel that the defence and military domain deserves their active and voluntary participation, even in times of emergency. Second, the oil state in Saudi Arabia (and its neighbours) is founded upon a patriarchal conception of the role of the ruler and the ruled: the regime is the source of prosperity and social welfare, in return for which the people implicitly leave the government to decide and carry out policies without consultation.

The combination of this psychological dependency with the potent lure of materialism creates effective limits to expansion of the armed forces and security elements. Most Saudis simply do not see the attraction of a soldier's life, and those that do have been recruited already. Thus, periodic announcements of intentions to expand the armed forces significantly, such as in the aftermath of the Kuwait War, do not get very far. Even though applications to military academies in the Kingdom are vastly oversubscribed (it is said that the Saudi military academy had 21,000 applications for 300 places in 1999), it can be argued that this is a temporary spin-off of tightened economic circumstances rather than a groundswell of desire for a martial life.[18]

There are other social ramifications to increasing recruitment. The southern provinces are the most populous in the Kingdom, yet these areas have enjoyed less prosperity, are less represented in senior and visible positions, and for historical reasons are less integrated into the country. (Much the same is true of the rural, tribal northern border regions and other remote areas of the Kingdom). These areas already provide a high proportion of the security forces – particularly, it is said, in the various units of the Ministry of the Interior – as well as the armed forces and the National Guard.[19] Any expansion of the armed forces would thus entail an increased proportion of southerners, and the regime is unlikely to see this as acceptable. And, given the government's hesitation even to tinker with utility subsidies, it is extremely unlikely that it would resort to stern measures such as conscription.

Saudi citizens' concerns

It should not be surprising that most Saudi citizens are more concerned with domestic issues than international ones, even those of national security. This is true in most countries. But the opinion of many Saudis that their government and rulers are losing touch with the needs, demands and wishes of their people is an extremely serious development, as it strikes at the heart of the regime's legitimacy. Furthermore, this feeling is increasingly entwined with a belief that the regime's security policies are designed, with Western connivance, more for regime survival than to meet the country's real needs.

Popular concern in Saudi Arabia centres on such issues as the following:

1. *Economic difficulties.* Most people recognise that the dizzy heights of prosperity achieved in the 1970s and early 1980s will never be reached again. Yet more than a dozen years of budget deficits, the translation of development projects into recurring budget items, and the cost of paying off the Kuwait War have all meant that the size of the economic pie has shrunk considerably, no matter what oil prices do in the foreseeable future.[20]

2. *Increased personal indebtedness.* The heyday of materialism may have been short-lived, but its impact lives on: the desire for consumer items – new cars, travel, satellite television – means that many people find themselves living beyond their means. Whereas at the height of Saudi Arabia's economic boom per capita income was on a par with that of the United States, at the start of the twenty-first century it had dropped to some $7,000 per year, relegating the country to Third World

status with correspondingly poor distribution of wealth and widening income disparity.[21]

3.   *Population growth.* Population growth rates in the GCC are said to be as high as 4%, and, even with its recent reduction, Saudi Arabia's is still far too high. The immediate problem is the need for heavy government expenditure on such items as health care and education for the majority of the population under the age of 16. Growing populations also mean heavier use of scarce resources and services, such as water and electricity.

4.   *Unemployment.* The long-term consequence of population growth is lack of jobs. This is already serious in Saudi Arabia, Bahrain and Oman. The Kingdom produces some 175,000 secondary-school graduates every year, yet there are jobs for only one in three Saudis seeking employment. The problem grows worse with every passing year.[22]

5.   *Continuing high-level corruption.* Since the 1980s the economic pie has shrunk, yet ruling families and allied elites appear to make no concessions over what they feel is their due. Hence, their standard of living remains unchanged or has risen, while that of most citizens has been declining. Corruption in all its forms has become a burning issue at all levels of society.

6.   *Wasted financial resources.* Public reaction is particularly hostile to arms purchases of almost any sort, to luxury and/or status projects undertaken by the state, and to other perceived non-essentials. 'White elephants' are singled out as symbols of ostentation and abuse of public funds.

7.   *Strife over women's roles and gender relations.* Traditionally, public roles for women have been among the most restricted in the world, but the boom in education, economy and government structure has created opportunities that women throughout the Gulf have slowly used to their advantage. While many men in Saudi Arabia have the same attitudes to women as their grandfathers, many others – typically younger and more educated – wish wives to work, are prepared to give women equal political rights. Unfortunately, the debate over women's rights seems to have become a focus for the struggle between liberals and Islamists.[23]

8.   *Inequities in social structure.* In part, the net effect of the oil revolution in the Gulf has been to reduce distinctions between

social and economic groups because of increased social mobility, education and economic opportunities. More importantly, however, it has also widened divides between them as the rich and privileged prosper while many citizens remain trapped in low-paying jobs and limited financial means. This has caused resentment in various states (most dramatically in Bahrain, where the unrest of the 1990s was fundamentally driven by economic grievances overlaid by social divisions). In the Kingdom, significant and troubling differences remain between *inter alia* Najdis and Hijazis, the rural north and south of the country and the more urbanized centre, and the Shiite minority (mostly found in the Eastern Province) and the rest of the country.

9.   *Questions of identity*. Expatriates form some 25% of Saudi Arabia's population. The question of national identity surfaces when Saudis must speak English to Indians and Filipinos in shops, when children learn nursery stories and legends from Sri Lankan nannies, and when political attitudes are shaped in schools by northern Arab teachers. Dependence on expatriates becomes mixed with resentment in the minds of the growing legion of young unemployed Saudis.

National security and relations between rulers and ruled

The legitimacy of Saudi Arabia's rulers rests upon a social compact that depends partly on a traditional, patriarchal foundation and partly on their managing the state so as to provide for the economic and social well-being of the citizenry. But as the population expands, so government becomes more complex, the ruling family grows more distant from the ruled and the regime's legitimacy faces an increasing danger of erosion. The regime is reluctant to undertake meaningful political reform, and its failure to respond to popular demand, no matter how muted at present, invites alienation. Most senior members of the Al Saud are aware of the problem. However, they are also on the horns of a dilemma: they seek to preserve their state and their position through alliance with the United States and the West, yet an increasing proportion of their population objects to American and Western policies in the region. The imbroglio since 11 September has strained the American–Saudi relationship and has undoubtedly subjected Saudi Arabia's domestic political framework to similar stress. The muttered opposition to American policies and vague expressions of support for America's enemies today may produce widespread criticism of the stewardship of the Al Saud tomorrow.

There are numerous reasons why the internal dimension of Saudi security is significant. First, there is a clear and urgent need for the present regime to manage effectively the political transitions a changing society requires. The patriarchal Saudi state must embrace progressive liberalisation and popular participation in the decision-making process – and sooner rather than later. Second, the regime must somehow come to terms with the sharpening tension between its dependence on the American relationship and popular discontent with American policies. In part, this seems to be the path that Prince Abdullah is following, but much will depend upon the direction of succession after him.

Third, one aspect of the emerging discord between rulers and ruled over foreign policy and security goals is the Gulf's failure to generate a genuine indigenous debate on, and conceptualisation of, Gulf security. This failure is the direct result of the closed nature of Gulf (and especially Saudi) politics. Many key issues of popular concern are not covered by the media and only cautiously raised in private conversation. There are few counterparts of Western research institutes and 'think tanks', and almost all of those that do exist are controlled by governments. As a result, publication and other dissemination of information and ideas deals with only acceptable subjects and takes place along regime-sanctioned lines. A freer environment for debate and discussion in Saudi Arabia might well produce a concept of Saudi and Gulf security dramatically different from the present one.

Chapter 3

The impact of 11 September 2001

It may be no exaggeration to note that, after the United States, Saudi Arabia was one of the countries most directly affected by the tragic events of 11 September 2001. The presumed mastermind behind the perpetrators was Saudi-born Osama bin Laden, and 15 of the 19 hijackers of the airliners involved were Saudis. In the initial months after the strikes, the Kingdom found itself under a barrage of verbal attacks by American commentators, and there were real fears of severe damage to Saudi–American relations.

The damage caused to Saudi society – by the abrupt discovery of the extent to which extremism subsisted within, and (among the educated at least) by the shock of the vitriolic attacks from outside – will be deeper and will take time to assess. Saudi credibility was severely damaged in the eyes of American popular opinion, as the spate of Saudi-bashing in the last quarter of 2001 proved. But, despite the marked tension, Saudi–American relations remain too important to both sides to be allowed to deteriorate.

The Saudi government, prominent members of the ruling family, the media and key religious leaders all condemned the attacks of 11 September. King Fahd, in an interview on the eve of the annual GCC summit, was quoted as saying 'It is normal that we cooperate to eradicate [terrorism] and ward off its evils'.[1] The Heir Apparent, Prince Abdullah bin Abd al-Aziz, declared at the summit that 'our Arab and Muslim nation was severely damaged because of the reckless acts of murderers who raised the banners of Islam … and claimed to fight for the Arab and Muslim nation, which was the first victim of their crimes … It is the duty of all Muslims in these circumstances to condemn all terrorist acts, without ambiguity'.[2]

In the absence of public opinion polls, the reaction of the Saudi public cannot be ascertained. But an opinion poll published in Kuwait on 19 November 2001 showed that 82% of Kuwaitis polled were opposed to the American attack on Afghanistan, and 89% felt that the attacks would lead to a further struggle, although 71% approved of their government's cooperation in the US 'war against terrorism'. At the same time, however, 42% viewed Osama bin Laden as a *mujahid* (holy warrior), while only 34% saw him as a terrorist.[3] Presumably, the opinions of the Saudi public were not markedly dissimilar.[4]

More importantly for American foreign policy, the regime repeatedly signalled its desire to continue strategic cooperation. The Saudis place great stress on the partnership. Unfortunately for the formation of American popular opinion, much of that cooperation, as usual, is carried out quietly, giving the appearance of Saudi inactivity or, worse, non-cooperation. The attitude of the Saudi government was that the close American–Saudi relationship had not been diminished or jeopardised, despite the differences over these foreign and security policy issues. Disagreements always have been part of the relationship – just as trade disputes form part of the broad US–European relationship.

Saudi Arabia and Islamic extremism

The events of late 2001 demonstrated that the relationship between Saudi Arabia and Islam also had its dark side. The involvement of numerous Saudis amongst the forces of Islamic terrorism inevitably will lead to some degree of introspection in the Kingdom and to examining the circumstances that gave birth to domestic Islamic extremism.

The great majority of Saudis are *Muwahhidun*, better known in the West as Wahabis.[5] The movement was founded in the eighteenth century by religious reformer Muhammad Abd al-Wahhab, who preached a return to the original austerity and purity of Islam. He also formed an alliance with the head of the Al Saud clan, which led to the extension of Al Saud power over much of the Arabian Peninsula with the aim of spreading the Wahabi message. The task of cementing Al Saud control over the present territory of the Kingdom fell to King Abd al-Aziz (often known in the West as Ibn Saud) in the first three decades of the twentieth century. In the early years of this process, Abd al-Aziz relied for much of his military force upon the Ikhwan, groups of Najdi tribesmen imbued with a strong sense of Wahabi duty.

Forced to recognise the limits to expansion posed by the British mandates of Transjordan and Iraq to the north and by the British-protected emirates of the Gulf to the east, King Abd al-Aziz was forced to abandon his strategy of spreading the reach of Wahabism and to concentrate instead on forging an emerging nation-state. But Abd al-Aziz's change of strategy brought him into direct conflict with the ultra-conservative wing of Wahabism and the Ikhwan. Although he faced off the Ikhwan and forced them to bow to his will, the seeds were sown for the continuing tension between the state under Al Saud leadership and strict interpreters of the Wahabi message. The persistence of the fanaticism of the Ikhwan was demonstrated in 1979, when a neo-Ikhwan group led by Juhayman al-Utaybi seized control of the Great Mosque of Mecca.[6]

It is one of the enduring myths of Western critics of Saudi Arabia that the Al Saud and the Saudi state are unidimensionally arch-conservative and reactionary. On the contrary, the successors of King Abd al-Aziz continue to walk a tightrope between respecting tradition and pursuing development. They have been forced to tread warily and slowly in introducing such innovations as radio, television and mass education. In 1965 the erection of a television transmitter in Riyadh provoked a demonstration that the police dispersed, but several were killed; ten years later the brother of one of those killed (and a member of the ruling family) assassinated King Faisal. In another example, the state eventually reached agreement with the *ulama* that girls should be educated – but control of female education was placed in the hands of the *ulama* through the General Presidency for Girls' Education.[7] In a game of give-and-take, the price King Fahd paid for grudging acceptance of his pursuit of development was the appointment of an arch-conservative, Sheikh Abd al-Aziz bin Baz, as *mufti* – a position signifying the highest religious authority in the country.

However, in tandem with a recrudescence of traditional Wahabi opposition to change in the Kingdom (as represented by those who took over the Great Mosque), other neo-traditionalist religious opposition began to appear in the 1970s. The *Salafiyah*, a term denoting a desire to return to the golden age of the Prophet

Muhammad, not only dismissed the Saudi state as corrupt and un-Islamic and opposed the Western presence in Saudi Arabia and the Islamic world, but also regarded the official religious establishment as a co-opted, and thus illegitimate, tool of the state. In the 1980s this opposition included figures such as Sheikh Abdullah bin Sulayman al-Masari, founder of the Committee for the Defence of Legitimate Rights (more accurately translated as Committee for the Defence of Sharia [Islamic law] Rights), and his son Muhammad, who represented the CDLR in exile in London along with Sa'd al-Faqih before the two quarrelled and split. In the 1990s Sheikhs Safar al-Hawali and Salman al-Awdah became known for their fiery sermons delivered in mosques in al-Qasim region of central Arabia.[8] Not surprisingly, some of these dissidents were vocal in their opposition to the American attack on Afghanistan.[9]

The best-known Islamic dissident of Saudi origin is, of course, Osama bin Laden. Disowned by the Saudi government and forced out of Sudan, Osama made his way to Afghanistan in 1996.[10] By this time, the tentacles of his al-Qaeda movement appear to have stretched to a number of countries, notably Egypt and Yemen, as well as Saudi Arabia. Although the specifics are hazy, Osama seems to have had close ties with the Aden-Abyan Islamic Army in southern Yemen, which kidnapped a group of tourists in December 1998. A number of their captives were killed in a firefight with Yemeni soldiers, and the head of the 'army' was tried in Yemeni courts, convicted and executed. But adherents, many of them 'Arab Afghans', remained at large in remote areas of the country. It is widely thought that some of them, in conjunction with Osama bin Laden, were responsible for the bomb attack on the American destroyer, USS *Cole*, in Aden harbour in September 2000. The four Saudis executed for the November 1995 bombing of a building in Riyadh used by an American training team for the Saudi Arabian National Guard, killing five Americans and two Indians, claimed to be influenced by Muhammad al-Masari and Osama bin Laden.[11]

It is clear from the 11 September hijackings that Osama had acquired a number of Saudi adherents: 15 of the 19 hijackers were of Saudi nationality. A significant number of the Saudis involved came from the southern and western regions of the Kingdom, areas that traditionally have nursed grievances against the central region of Najd, home of the ruling Al Saud family, and have benefited relatively less from oil income.[12] In addition, at least 45 Saudis were killed in the 2001 war in Afghanistan,[13] and at least 240 more Saudis were captured.[14] The number of Saudis recruited by al-Qaeda to defend Islam in what were regarded locally as 'just wars' is an indication not of the Saudi government's passivity but rather of a failure of its intelligence and of its judgment in assigning low priority to this problem.

Unlike the previous Saudi religious critics, Osama bin Laden and his comrades and followers seem to cleave to a more ecumenical and activist Islamist ideology – not necessarily Wahabi, or even Sunni, but one that seeks to appeal to all Muslims. Hence his alliance with Ayman al-Zawahiri, the Egyptian founder of Islamic Jihad in Egypt, and his appeal to 'Arab Afghans' from many countries. He is also distinguished by his insistent opposition to the US military presence in the Arabian Peninsula and by his uncompromising advocacy of violence to achieve his aims. Ideologically, Osama descends from the extreme reactionary branch of Salafi Islamic revivalism that first appeared over a century ago. While many dissident Wahabi activists may agree with some or much of Osama's invective, they are unlikely to regard him as their leader. And, although Osama's Saudi origins cannot be dismissed as entirely insignificant in his ideological evolution, his ideology clearly does not derive from either Saudi liberal or traditionalist positions. In many respects, he might as well have been an Egyptian, Algerian or Yemeni.[15]

A new campaign of Saudi-bashing and the Saudi response

One of the more alarming side-effects of 11 September was the emergence of a new round of Saudi-bashing in the United States. The Kingdom had long been regarded with suspicion or hostility by some Americans for any number of reasons: it has been blamed for high oil prices; it supports the establishment of a Palestinian state and thus is a foe of Israel; it was seen as uncooperative with the American investigation into the 1996 al-Khobar bombing; it is not a Western-style democracy; it insists on the segregation of women; and it suffers from a widespread stereotype that its population consists of ignorant Bedouins who undeservedly have traded their camels for Cadillacs. After 11 September 2001, though, hostility to Saudi Arabia intensified, largely because most of the hijackers appeared to be Saudis and because of a popular perception, stoked by the mainstream media, that the Saudis were not doing their part in the American 'war against terror', after President Bush's warning that 'Either you are with us, or you are with the terrorists'.[16]

In the US the last months of 2001 were marked by an intensive programme of detention of largely Middle Eastern suspects, including a number of Saudis.[17] The seemingly indiscriminate nature of the dragnet, the refusal to release information on detainees and the denial of access for defence lawyers sparked civil-liberty concerns and fears of anti-Arab racism.[18] One prominent case involved a Saudi doctor studying in San Antonio, who was arrested and kept in solitary confinement for 13 days simply because his name was similar to those of some of the hijackers.[19] A Muslim Arab-American Secret Service agent, on his way to Texas to provide protection for US President George W. Bush, was removed from an American Airlines plane he had already boarded.[20] Even a US Congressman of Arab descent, a member of a congressional delegation on its way to Saudi Arabia, was bounced from an Air France flight in Paris.[21] By early 2002 only 44 of the Saudis held by the US government had been released.[22]

Otherwise responsible media were full of anti-Saudi polemics, some scholars contended that Islam and Saudi Arabia were intrinsic threats to the West, and the mayor of New York rejected a prominent Saudi businessman's humanitarian gesture of a $10m cheque for relief because he objected to his politics. Members of the United States Congress also made inflammatory statements. An American senator accused the Saudis of playing a 'double game' of giving extremists free rein at home and financing their groups.[23] The chairman of the Senate Foreign Relations Committee claimed that Saudi schools were 'hate-filled anti-American breeding grounds'.[24] Another senator, chairman of the Armed Services Committee, suggested that the United States should withdraw its military forces from the Kingdom to 'a place which has not seen significant resources flowing to support some really extreme, fanatic views'.[25] Former CIA Director James Woolsey contended that Saudi Arabia 'deserves a very large part of the blame for September 11. I do not think we should do anything more with them right now than be cordial'.[26]

The media reported that the Saudis had refused to arrest any of the suspects identified by the US government – although this was shown to be false.[27] The media also claimed that Saudi Arabia failed to close bank accounts used by individuals and organisations linked to al-Qaeda. The Saudi response was slow, in part because of the government's claim that Washington had failed to provide evidence of the linkages or even advance warning of publicly announced lists of suspected terrorists and their organisations, but action was forthcoming.[28] Another media claim was that the Saudis had refused to allow American use of its military facilities for its Afghanistan campaign, including the American-run command centre at Prince Sultan Air Base outside al-Kharj. Little heed was paid to official Saudi and American statements that the US government had never asked to base aircraft used in Afghanistan at Saudi bases, and that the US military did indeed use the Prince Sultan command centre to direct the war.[29] Nevertheless, some members of Congress and the media continued to contend that Saudi Arabia was dragging its heels on cooperation in 'the war against terror'. Just as regularly, the White House countered that it had excellent cooperation with Riyadh.[30] One paper added fuel to the flames in early 2002 when it claimed that Saudi officials had hinted that Riyadh might ask for the removal of US troops in the country.[31] The Bush administration quickly dismissed the report, with denials by the White House spokesman, the Secretary of State, the Secretary of Defence, the Secretary of the Air Force, the Assistant Secretary of State for Political-Military Affairs and the Chairman of the Joint Chiefs of Staff. The Saudis also denied it.

Nevertheless, the media attacks appeared to have played a key role in shifting American public opinion against Saudi Arabia and other Arab countries. One opinion poll saw a drop in the US public's favourable view of Saudi Arabia from 56% to 24% between January 2001 and December 2001; over the same time, its unfavourable rating climbed from 28% to 58%.[32]

Are these allegations credible or simply incredible? First, rather than trying to push up oil prices, the Saudis (as well as many other members of OPEC) seek to maintain what they regard as a reasonable and stable price. Today's oil price in real terms is said to be less than it was before the oil price revolution in 1973–4.[33] The drop in crude oil prices to under $10 a barrel in 1998 and early 1999 (the price averaged slightly more than $13 for the whole of 1998), created severe budgetary problems for Saudi Arabia, which depends on oil for some 80% of its government income. In 2001 Riyadh recorded its first budgetary surplus for more than a decade, because the price of oil rose to levels between $25 and $30. With the drop in late 2001 and early 2002 to $20 a barrel or less (although recovering to about $25), the budgets of Saudi Arabia and other OPEC producers went back into the red, and development efforts had to be postponed or curtailed. Simply put, this cannot be called price gouging, and it is in the interest of both the Kingdom and the West that oil prices stay within a band around a mutually agreed optimal price, generally defined as $25 a barrel.[34]

Second, the establishment of a Palestinian state is a central goal throughout the Arab world and enjoys significant support around the world. Riyadh's official stance is that a Palestinian state must be created on the territories occupied by Israel in 1967, and that the Oslo process is the best way to achieve a lasting peace between Israel and its neighbours.[35] In the absence of more systematic research, anecdotal evidence suggests that most of its citizens seem to support that position. Now that the United States officially has accepted the principle of Palestinian statehood, this is hardly an extreme demand.

The Saudi complaint about al-Khobar, as well as about events after 11 September, has been that the US government systematically has failed to share information and evidence. There are also hints that the FBI has been heavy-handed and over-zealous in its activities in the Kingdom, and a similar charge has been made in connection with the USS *Cole* investigation in neighbouring Yemen.[36] Certainly the Saudis are not blameless in this affair: Saudi security services have never been noted for their cooperation with other forces and have often been over-the-top in their treatment of Saudi citizens and especially expatriates. At the same time, however, the handing down of indictments in the case in June 2001 a few days before the expiry of the statute of limitations, as well as the retirement of FBI Director Louis Freeh, without any prior notice to the Saudis and without the presentation of credible evidence, was regarded as an affront in Riyadh.[37] Essentially, the Saudis resent America's arrogance in seeming to believe that it can run these investigations as it likes, without regard to Saudi sovereignty.

It is certainly true that Saudi Arabia is not a Western-style democracy. It is also undeniable that the Al Saud ruling family often acts as if the country belongs to it alone. And the political system is authoritarian. But the regime is more accurately described as patriarchal, rather than tyrannical. Far from opposing change and denying basic rights to its citizens, the government has promoted steady economic and social change – albeit at a measured pace, so as to keep a workable balance between traditionalists and modernists within the Kingdom. While the King and close family members make final decisions, a highly educated senior government cadre, drawn from diverse backgrounds, has come to play a key role in the decision-making process. The *majlis* system, under which many princes, governors, government officials and prominent business-men host regular sessions that all are welcome to attend to voice comments and complaints, provides valuable feedback, even if sensitive topics are proscribed. Furthermore, the establishment of a formal *Majlis al-Shura*, although long in coming, is in itself an indicator of political transition. Anecdotal evidence again suggests that most Saudis do not want a different political system; they just want the present system to be fairer and more responsive.

The practice differentiating the Kingdom from nearly every country in the world, including its neighbours in the GCC, is its rigid segregation of women from men. This does not mean that its treatment of women is the same as that of the Taliban; although women in the Kingdom must be cloaked, and indigenous women must be veiled, most are educated, many work, a large number travel abroad and some run their own businesses.[38] It is arguable that female segregation is due more to social constraint than deliberate government policy, and that the government has been loosening the shackles at the same necessarily slow rate as in many other fields. In the end, however, the truth is that Saudi Arabia can learn more in this regard from its neighbours from Kuwait to Oman, where women drive, study and work side-by-side with men, hold high government positions and are eloquent in public participation.

It is unarguable that Wahabism is a conservative expression of Islam, and that Saudi Arabia's long isolation from outside influences, its historical development and pressures of its development have strengthened the hand of Wahabi traditionalists. But this is a long way from contending that Saudi Arabia supports and foments extremism. Pious Saudis, and the government to some extent, have engaged in Wahabi proselytising efforts around the world – but then many Christian groups also proselytise abroad, among them offshoots more extreme than the Wahabis. Undoubtedly, the Saudi establishment in Riyadh and Jeddah has realised, rather belatedly, that unsupervised religious activities can make fertile territory for a few extremists, and that serious soul-searching is in order over how to separate the twisted extremists from the responsibly devout.

Are the Saudis really ignorant Bedouin driving Cadillacs? No, of course not. A minority is rich, as in America and Europe. Some members of this minority regard their fortune as a licence to do whatever they like, but others are competent, responsible businessmen who donate to charitable causes, as is required in Islam. Many are educated, middle-class people. They drive Fords and Toyotas as well as Mercedes, they work in government offices or for corporations or as small businessmen; they seek loans to build their houses and promotions to provide for their children. Many Saudis are relatively poor, live in modest housing and earn incomes as drivers and soldiers. Instead of being rich, a growing proportion are simply unemployed. Are Saudis anti-American? Undoubtedly some are, but many are absorbed with American culture even if they disagree with aspects of America's foreign policy.

The 11 September attacks and the American war in Afghanistan are likely to have substantial impact on the Kingdom's policies, but the dire warnings advanced in Western media that Saudi Arabia is on the verge of collapse are the stuff of fantasy. The same sort of predictions of doom have been advanced at various intervals since the 1940s. First, it was said that the nascent state, full of regional rivalries and overwhelmed by its inability to manage the new phenomenon of oil income, could not outlast the death of King Abd al-Aziz. A decade later, the Kingdom was seen as tottering because of the incompetence and profligacy of King Saud in the 1950s. Later it was contended that the Kingdom was helpless to withstand the challenge of Arab nationalism in the 1960s, particularly with Nasser's Egyptian forces poised in strength on Saudi Arabia's Yemen frontier. The fall of the Shah of Iran in the late 1970s brought predictions that the Al Saud would soon suffer the same fate, and the collapse of oil prices in the mid-1980s was seen as another final nail in the Saudi coffin. In the 1990s the rise and visibility of Islamic critics of the regime, both inside and outside the country, brought new fears that the Kingdom's days were numbered.[39]

Certainly, the Kingdom faces serious problems – in corruption, in the unchecked arrogance of the Al Saud, in growing socio-economic difficulties and so on. But Saudi Arabia is not quite the dinosaur that the instant experts in the West seem to think. The state has grown more sophisticated in dealing with these problems. With regard to 11 September, the government swiftly took precautions to make certain that domestic religious dissent did not get out of hand.[40]

Adjustments to the events of 2001 cannot be predicted, of course. But likely effects may well include one or more of the following:

1. The government is likely to exercise closer supervision and tighter control over the international Muslim organisations headquartered within the Kingdom. It may well reassess and place stricter controls on the direction of its parallel Islamic foreign policy, although it is unlikely to regard official policies of building mosques and distributing Korans as subject to revision.

2. The state will undoubtedly seek closer control of domestic Islamists, via intensified penetration of and restrictions on Islamist groups and individuals, as well as via less tolerance of deviation from official viewpoints. This may well have the unintended side effect of increasing Islamist dissent among disaffected elements and driving it further underground and outside the country. On the other hand, it may well give the liberals a slight edge in the unending balancing of modernist aspirations against traditionalist obstructionism. Possibly this has been signalled already in the newly instituted issue of identity cards for women and in the tantalising promises that in the near future women may be allowed to drive motor vehicles.[41]

3. The regime undoubtedly will be far more meticulous in keeping track of Saudi citizens who leave the country to join Islamic causes in such places as Bosnia, Chechnya and Kashmir. Still, just as Riyadh (and Washington) was not aware of the involvement of the Saudi hijackers of 11 September, it will prove difficult to prevent and/or detain such activists.

4. In the short run, it is likely that official relations with the United States will cool slightly, particularly if there is no progress on the Israeli–Palestinian front and the US continues its uncompromising support of Israel. On the popular level, the United States may expect to see a short-term decline in the number of Saudi visitors, students and investments. These are more likely to be temporary dips rather than long-term consequences.[42] The picture will radically change, however, should hints about military action against Iraq become facts.[43] Public opinion in

Saudi Arabia, not to mention all the Gulf states and the entire Arab world, has become convinced that ten years of United Nations sanctions have had no effect on Saddam Hussein and his policies, but have served only to bring suffering to the Iraqi people.[44]

5.   Saudi insistence on sovereignty is likely to mean stiffer Saudi resolve on retaining jurisdiction over suspects in the 1996 al-Khobar bombing and, especially, any extradition of 11 September suspects (particularly in the absence of US explanation or apology for detaining Saudi citizens).

6.   Ties to Islamic countries, especially Pakistan, are likely to be strengthened. Given its perceived role as the protector of Islam, the Kingdom will find it necessary to deal with the increasing suspicion throughout the Islamic world that Islam is under attack from the West.

Without a doubt, the last months of 2001 and the early ones of 2002 have been trying times for the Kingdom – as well as for some of its fellow GCC members. It has seen a Saudi by birth become the most hated man on earth. It has discovered that Islamic extremists inside the Kingdom and its extremist citizens abroad pose far more of a threat than it supposed, and that real change must be made to disarm this threat. It has found itself the target of American hostility on a scale never seen before, leading to the real possibility that the 70-year American–Saudi alliance (the Kingdom's closest bond outside the Arab world) will be jeopardised. While the long-term damage may be limited, the more immediate impact on Saudi policy makers and general population alike may be to rethink their overwhelmingly pro-Western and pro-American attitudes.

The Saudi–American relationship: the circle and the square

Saudi Arabia, very consciously, has deepened its 'special relationship' with the United States over the years. It is a relationship with many facets, both official and popular. In part, it is based on a long history of Saudi–American ties, particularly the establishment of the Arabian-American Oil Company (ARAMCO), originally a consortium made up of five American oil companies. ARAMCO received the first oil concession for the Kingdom and served as its principal producing company for many years. But ARAMCO's role extended far beyond the oil industry proper. It employed many Saudis in its operations; it educated many more; and it encouraged the establishment of a multitude of local companies from which it could make in-country purchases. It provided advice and counsel to Saudi kings and government. It created the first archive of historical materials and place-names in the country. And it was nationalised by the Saudi government almost reluctantly, years later than elsewhere in OPEC.

The ARAMCO relationship was soon mirrored on a political level, and then on a military level as well. The political relationship was regarded as particularly important during the 1950s and 1960s, when the Kingdom found itself under attack from the Arab nationalist republics. During the Cold War, the Kingdom's staunch anti-communist attitude struck a common chord with US administrations. The military association began with the establishment of the Dhahran air base, which was operated by the US Air Force between 1946 and 1962, and the provision of an American training team from 1953. Military ties escalated considerably in subsequent years and remain extremely significant.

Ties are also evident on a more personal level. American pop culture is extremely popular amongst a wide swathe of Saudi youth. Aspects of the American consumer culture, from Starbucks to McDonalds to American-style shopping malls and American cars, are everywhere. The thousands of Saudis who studied in the United States proclaim nostalgic memories of their stay there, and many retain homes in and/or travel to the US.

But there are undeniable cracks in hitherto close bilateral relations, and they are growing wider. The intensification of US popular and elite suspicions of Saudi Arabia after 11 September 2001 is damaging. New myths of Saudi intolerance in education and of its propagation of extremist Islamic views abroad have been superimposed on existing stereotypes. Saudis bristle at a perceived anti-Arab, and particularly anti-Saudi, attitude in some quarters in the United States, especially in the media and the Congress. If these attitudes continue, the end result is likely to be increasing numbers of Saudi citizens choosing other destinations for their holidays, education, property purchases and investment. It may also mean less fluid cooperation on military matters and adverse repercussions on trade. Such a deterioration will damage not only Saudi interests but American interests as well.

The Saudi government is frustrated at difficulties over its application for membership in the World Trade Organisation (WTO). Many Saudi officials attribute the obstacles to gaining admission to behind-the-scenes US manoeuvres, while many American officials insist that participation in the WTO requires more competition in Saudi Arabia's economy and more transparency in its government. Furthermore, there are growing perceptions that the United States is displaying increasing arrogance during the post-Cold War era. Rather than negotiating and persuading Saudi Arabia and the Gulf states to cooperate in security and political matters, the US is seen as simply telling its clients what they must do. This behaviour seems to have increased in the last quarter of 2001 and the beginning of 2002.

In the wider arena, divergence of views over Iraq threatens military cooperation. The Kingdom strongly resists US pressure to support what appears to be an increasingly aggressive anti-Iraq policy. As pointed out above, the Kingdom's leaders do not trust Saddam Hussein, nor can they work with him. At the same time, though, they strongly oppose military action to remove him. Minister of the Interior Prince Nayif bin Abd al-Aziz responded to a question about an attack on Iraq at a press conference in mid-February 2002 by saying that 'Saudi Arabia is against resolving disputes through violence ... If this happens, God forbid, the Kingdom will not in any circumstance be for any war against any Arab country'.[45] The body of Saudi population is even more antagonistic to an assault on Iraq. An American assault on Iraq, even if only remotely similar to the campaign in Afghanistan, stands a good chance by itself of derailing the strategic and military side of Saudi–US cooperation.

The inclusion of Iran in the Bush administration's 'axis of evil' blacklist confounds the Saudis. The biggest power on the Gulf littoral, Iran is only a few miles away across the Gulf, and the Saudis know full well that, at a minimum, an essential part of their security rests on achieving a *modus vivendi* with the Islamic Republic. Rational self-interest has dictated Riyadh's gradual rapprochement with Tehran. It is in Saudi interests to strengthen ties in many ways beyond a simple normalisation of relations. American hostility to Iran, particularly when not immediately provoked, complicates Saudi–Iranian relations and jeopardises whatever influence the Saudis may have in encouraging Iranian moderates.

There is no greater source of permanent rancour between the two countries than the imbroglio of Palestine. The deep passions on the subject at all levels of Saudi society dictate that the Kingdom's fundamental support for the Palestinian cause will not diminish. The longer the present cycle of violence and hatred continues, the more it will poison US relations, not only with Saudi Arabia but with the entire Arab world and the Middle East. If the United States continues to remain essentially disengaged and at least passively supports the Sharon government in its tough line, the possibility exists that the Kingdom will move beyond verbal remonstrations and take direct action against the United States. Prince Abdullah has publicly ruled out another oil boycott, but there are other potential measures short of that drastic step.

All the Gulf regimes have serious reservations about the perceived American slant towards Israel, and increasingly voice their protest. They feel indignation themselves and/or feel they must act on the indignation of their people regarding American policies towards Israel and Iraq. The Saudi heir apparent and *de facto* head of government, Prince Abdullah, spoke with frustration in June 2001 when on a visit to Syria he stated that

> *the premises and given facts of peace implemented since the conference in Madrid are now crumbling one by one. The Madrid conference received the acceptance of the Arabs and the Muslims, who extended the bridges of dialogue, hoping that this would bring about a future of co-existence for all parties according to the principles of justice and land for peace. This vision from Madrid is what led the Arabs to shake hands with Israeli negotiators, even though for more than fifty years they had rejected the extending of a friendly hand to any Israeli party. Today, what has happened to Madrid and its commitments, and what about the peace process in all its forms?*[46]

In August 2001 he was angry enough to send an unusually sharp letter to President Bush airing his concerns. The President of the United Arab Emirates, Sheikh Zayid bin Sultan Al Nahyan, remarked on 3 July 2001 that 'At a time Israel unleashes its lethal weapons against the Palestinian people who have nothing else but stones, we see the United States unable to rein in Israel.'[47] Even after the 11 September attacks, Saudi officials continued to voice their concern over Israeli–Palestinian developments.[48] The Israeli offensive into West Bank towns in early 2002 redoubled Saudi official dismay and intensified public outrage against Israel and the United States, provoking rare public demonstrations in the kingdom and elsewhere in the Gulf.

Prince Abdullah was widely praised for advancing an Arab–Israeli peace plan promising full normalisation of relations in exchange for the return of territory, which was adopted by an Arab League summit on 28 March 2002. His visit to President Bush's ranch in Texas in late April, during which the prince presented a new Arab–Israeli peace strategy, was useful in forging a personal bond and nudging Bush towards more engagement on the problem. This positive development, however, was undermined by the negative reaction of Western public opinion to the near-simultaneous incidents involving the death of 15 girls during a Mecca school fire because the local religious police prevented them from leaving without being properly dressed and the publication of a poem by the Saudi ambassador to London that appeared to praise a female Palestinian suicide bomber.

Another source of divergence, differences over policy towards other Arab states, has diminished in recent years. Although the US has toned down its attitude to regimes in Libya and Syria, any change in US policy will be robustly resisted by Saudi Arabia. The Kingdom remains suspicious of Qaddafi but fully supportive of Syria.

Observers in the West have often made much of Prince Abdullah's 'Arab' orientation relative to the Al Fahd, the branch of the family comprising King Fahd and his full-brothers, who are often regarded as closer to the US. Inevitably, this supposed divergence has taken on far too much significance. But with the steady deterioration in the Palestinian–Israeli situation, it is not inconceivable that Abdullah might feel constrained to use stronger means to express disapproval of US support for Israel than simply postponing a visit to the United States, as he did in mid-2001. One possibility might be to diversify arms purchases and training programmes more clearly in favour of other suppliers. The unofficial boycott of American products such as Coca Cola and Burger King, begun in sympathy with the second *intifada*, might conceivably evolve into more red tape and hassle over importing American goods, especially if the Saudis continue to feel thwarted over their country's delayed WTO membership.

Should Saudi–American relations be reduced to a worst-case scenario involving the termination or drastic rescaling of the 'special relationship', does the Kingdom have other options to underpin its security efforts and economic prosperity? Could a new, exclusive relationship be built with Western Europe? Although the Kingdom could not expect to receive the same level of military protection that it enjoys with the US, European nations can and have provided significant assistance in the Gulf, as demonstrated in the Kuwait War. Britain's long relationship with all the GCC states generally has stood it in good stead with Gulf regimes. Moreover, Europe offers multiple investment opportunities – Europe–GCC trade already outstrips the trade with the US – and Gulf elites have strong personal ties to Europe. But there are negative aspects, ranging from simple matters, such as the difficulty of dealing with Europe as a single entity to trade problems, such as the inability of the GCC and Europe to reach agreement on petrochemical tariffs despite discussions lasting over a decade. And Western Europe can hardly be expected to side with Saudi Arabia should there be a serious dispute with the US.

Elsewhere, Russia has long been a player in the Gulf, although its support (notably for Iraq and Yemen) has most often run counter to the interests of Saudi Arabia and its Gulf allies. Bridges of cooperation and understanding would have to be built virtually from scratch, and the effort might not be worthwhile. Much of a half-century of military development, training and doctrine would have to be replaced, and the Saudi model of economic development inevitably would be altered. Moreover, the two countries are cut-throat competitors in the oil market; Russia cannot provide the sort of investment and export-import climate on which Saudi businesses depend; and Moscow is not in a position to go head to head with the US over what for it must be a marginal interest.

Although China, as a growing consumer of Gulf oil and gas, has even more immediate national interests in the Gulf, its attractiveness as a partner is limited. True, it has useful military hardware for sale (it already has sold some equipment to Saudi Arabia and Kuwait and could provide training and other assistance), but its economy is still developing, and the kind of expertise and trade it could offer is restricted. In addition, China does not have either the force-projection capabilities of even Russia, nor, seemingly, any interest in developing them *vis-à-vis* the Gulf. A Saudi switch to Chinese assistance would have serious negative consequences for Saudi security needs. In short, reliance on China is an even less viable choice than relying on Russia.

Is there any point in looking elsewhere? An integrated GCC is far too small and weak to assure its own security against external attack. A broader Gulf security pact with Iran and Iraq simply is not feasible under present circumstances, even if Iran and Iraq could be persuaded to cooperate with each other. Even broader Arab security agreements, depending only on understandings with other friendly Arab states, are not likely to be useful, as shown in the quiet death of the 'GCC plus two' (closer cooperation between the GCC and Egypt and Syria) scenario following the Kuwait War. Similarly, a far wider arrangement involving Islamic and/or Third World spheres is even more problematic. Over and above the obstacles to creating a workable alliance (how to get such essential components as India and Pakistan to cooperate together), there is the essential question of whether such allies would be able to prevent an attack on Saudi Arabia and the GCC, and (even more fundamentally) whether they would actually take action when required.

In short, in the foreseeable future there is no viable option for the Saudis other than to continue to depend on the United States and the West for their regional security concerns. It is also true that continuing the alliance with Saudi Arabia is a valuable option for the United States. But it is equally true that fundamental differences between the two countries make it imperative for the Kingdom to move beyond improvident dependence on the West and to design a more lasting strategy.

Despite the present level of cooperation with the West, Gulf regimes only partly share the Western conception that Gulf security depends on containing Iraq and Iran. Gulf regimes acquiesce in the Western definition of Gulf security and cooperate with Western policy arrangements for reasons of alliance maintenance and regime survival. They feel that their states are small and vulnerable and the objects of real or potential threats in a sea of hostility. Furthermore, they are afraid that external actors and/or events may jeopardise their position or result in their overthrow. They also fear that the West might abandon them unless they cooperate. More fundamentally, they have failed to conceptualise their own formulation of Gulf security, finding it easier to simply rely on outside forces to provide protection.

Regimes also worry about American long-term commitment to the Gulf. What will happen when the world no longer depends on the free flow of Gulf oil? They cite America's failure to stand behind the Shah of Iran when his regime was threatened; they point to American retreats from Lebanon and Somalia when their presence was attacked; and they have the earlier experience of abrupt British withdrawal from the Gulf without due consultation or consideration. They are uneasy about America's failure to consult with them on policies that affect them, and fear that their concerns and needs will be disregarded. All of these questions point to a deeper, fundamental concern that the most important considerations in regime survival may be internal, rather than external, and that complying with the American policy of containing Iraq and Iran may be more likely to threaten Gulf security than to protect it.

Conclusion

To what extent is Saudi security illusory? On the one hand, no country enjoys total security, and the Kingdom is certainly no exception. On the other, Saudi Arabia is seriously vulnerable to both internal and external pressures. The history of Saudi external security concerns indicates that explicit threats emerge, recede and are replaced by new threats in an almost cyclical pattern. Past success in withstanding these threats is no guarantee for the future, although the Kingdom does have a proven track record of withstanding them. But the enormous extent of fundamental internal change appears to be generating steadily increasing pressures on the country, the government and, especially, the ruling family and leadership.

This study of Gulf and Saudi security advances two specific and related conclusions. The first is longer-term or more fundamental: the need for an indigenous conceptualisation of Gulf security. The second is more medium-term: the Saudi–American relationship, upon which the Saudi regime has set so much store, has been damaged, possibly beyond full repair.

A policy of inclusion, not exclusion

Growing numbers of people in Saudi Arabia and the Gulf regard regional and even internal challenges as the most serious threats to Gulf security. They argue that effective and durable policy regarding Iraq and Iran must be based on inclusion rather than exclusion. Iraq and Iran are integral parts of the Gulf, and the Arab littoral must find productive ways of co-existing with the present regimes in those countries.

Policies of exclusion are counterproductive for a number of reasons. They do not achieve their desired goals: Saddam Hussein is still in power and following the same policies 11 years after the Kuwait War, and external pressure and sanctions have not forced regime change or adaptation in Iran. Moreover, generations of Iraqis and Iranians come to adulthood knowing only hostility from the West and also from the Gulf states, and, quite naturally, this creates in them a profound and long-term counter-hostility. Policies of exclusion hamper or prevent the very type of socio-economic development in the Gulf that promises to benefit all parties.

Policies of inclusion are desirable because they diminish or counteract the hostility, and hence the threats, of both regimes and populations in Iraq and Iran. Creating economic bonds between the Gulf states and Iraq and Iran holds the promise of binding the states together and rendering impotent hostile policies that cause damage on all sides.[1] Policies of inclusion make compromise solutions to disputes more likely.[2] They represent attempts to reach permanent solutions to current problems with the aim of fostering moderation and cooperation between states, rather than short-term strategies that use superior power to force recalcitrant regimes to alter policies.[3]

Furthermore, the divergence in Saudi Arabia between regime and popular views of Gulf security threatens to drive a wedge between rulers and ruled. Debate about the issue of Gulf security, which could potentially lead to the formulation of a Gulf or Saudi concept of Gulf security, is absent because the government inhibits free speech and resists meaningful political participation.

The old bases of the Saudi regime's legitimacy have been eroded due to such factors as the elaboration and complication of society, the increasing infiltration of external ideas,[4] the growing sophistication of the population, and the burgeoning intelligentsia. The Saudi regime is reluctant to permit or expand political participation, because it fears this will further erode legitimacy, undermine the privileged position of the ruling family and weaken the existing basis of state and society. But the regime's failure to recognise popular concerns and/or act upon them may lead to alienation. Public opinion is extremely exercised about the plight of both the Palestinians and the Iraqi people. Many Saudis are also concerned about the American war in Afghanistan and hints of further reprisals against Muslims elsewhere. The outbreak of demonstrations in Saudi Arabia and other Gulf states at the onset of the second *intifada*, as well as calls for the removal of Israeli trade missions in Gulf states and boycotts of American symbols such as McDonalds, was perceived by the regime as a threat to the public order. Vague expressions of support today for leaders like Saddam Hussein may lead to more substantial backing in the future. Actions such as demonstrations, public discussion and other activities focused on external events and policies may encourage similar expressions regarding internal policies

Conceptualisation of Gulf security and strategies is hampered because the government actively discourages debate by local media, institutes and other groups. Consequently, conceptions of Gulf security and strategies originate in Western policy making and think tanks; there is no independent conceptualisation in Saudi Arabia or the Gulf to reflect Gulf conceptions of Gulf security – this is a major reason why Gulf security formulations consider only external threats. While Western Gulf security formulations only consider the external environment, Saudi views of Gulf security include both internal and external threats, and even regard the internal threats as significantly more serious.

An indigenous conceptualisation of Gulf security may well reject the cornerstone principle of containment. Serious doubts are expressed at all levels of society about American resolve and motivations. Containment can only be a short- or medium-term strategy: it addresses static 'present-day' situations without providing or working towards offering fundamental solutions to the immediate political problems.

There is considerable reason to believe that Saudi Arabia's acquiescence in a Western-driven environment of containment is actually inimical to its long-term interests. If the present regime persists in following this avenue, there is a growing likelihood that relations with its population will be endangered, perhaps fatally. While in the foreseeable future there may be no alternative to partnership with the United States generally, and reliance on an American–Saudi security alliance in particular, Saudi Arabia's failure to develop an indigenous security strategy will almost certainly guarantee that the Kingdom will have no future choice but to follow the American lead, despite the costs.

The health of Saudi–US relations

For most of its history, the Kingdom of Saudi Arabia has placed extraordinary emphasis on its 'special relationship' with the United States, a relationship seen as instrumental in forging and shaping the country's socio-economic development and equally vital in assuring the Kingdom's security. But the long-standing partnership between Washington and Riyadh is showing increasing strains both in the wider strategic (or regional security) aspect and in bilateral relations.

Nevertheless, for Saudi Arabia there is no alternative to continuing its 'special relationship' with the US. And, if truth be told, there is little alternative for the United States either, without great cost. The most important reason for the US to save the relationship is undeniably the dominant position of Saudi Arabia in the world oil market. US imports of Saudi oil may be declining, but it should not be forgotten that the non-interruption of Saudi exports to Europe and especially Asia are also extremely important considerations in the American national interest.

There is, however, another important reason for the relationship, and one that goes beyond the simplistic dictum of 'security for oil'. The United States cannot afford to overlook the importance of Saudi Arabia as an ally and supporter in the region. The Kingdom is a convenient base for – as well as supporter of – regional operations, whether against Iraq, Iran, Afghanistan, Yemen, Somalia or wherever else US force might be needed in the unforeseeable future. Even more importantly, Saudi political influence in the Gulf, Arab and Islamic spheres is valuable to American foreign-policy objectives. The Saudi role is not one that can simply be replicated by the US acting on its own, and there are few actors in the region with the standing and broad ties that Riyadh offers.[5]

Change in Saudi Arabia is glacial: it may not be easy to see but it does exist, as a retrospective examination of the past six or seven decades will confirm. The Kingdom is in the midst of a period during which internal demands on and challenges to the existing system seem to be accelerating. Thus the West must recognise that a unique process of change exists in the Saudi environment and encourage its steady continuation where appropriate. The West should continue to support the economic liberalisation of Saudi Arabia and the Gulf states, not only for the prospective trade and investment benefits this will bring, but because the growing populations and small-sized economies in the Gulf will increasingly need steady economic diversification and growth in employment opportunities.

Economic change drives political perceptions. Any 'social contract' based on traditional relations between rulers and ruled in the Gulf is already dying. As society evolves, as economic opportunities become more restricted, and as citizens find themselves sharing less and less in the lifestyles and perceptions of ruling families, political change is as inevitable – and it will be difficult. Heavy-handed pressure on Saudi Arabia to create an elected parliamentary body is not appropriate. Gentle encouragement of such core concerns as free and constructive fora of debate on national issues and gradually freer treatment of women might be more proper and effective. On the Saudi side, expanding Western tourism along the lines followed by some of its GCC neighbours undoubtedly will bring benefits over and above additional income.

In terms of external security, policy makers in Washington and other Western capitals must realise that unilateral actions affecting the Gulf, the Middle East and the Islamic world have deep impacts on Saudi Arabia, the Gulf states and their people. American policies concerning Iraq and Iran should be based on full discussion and agreement with Riyadh and the GCC at the highest government levels. Military solutions can only have short-term impact and, without whole-hearted cooperation from the GCC states, will be more difficult and ephemeral in their results. Disengagement from the problem of deepening Israeli–Palestinian hostility (and from constructive dialogue with the Palestinian Authority) will continue to harm American interests in much of the world. The Kingdom may not be able to change American policy *vis-à-vis* Israel but it will find it necessary to create more distance between itself and the United States, even if it is only on this issue.

In the short to medium term, it is in the interests of both sides to repair and maintain a mutually beneficial relationship, even if it should mean significant loosening of the bonds and at least some Saudi acquiescence in an American policy of containment. Over the long-term, however, Saudi interests may be best served by nurturing a more indigenous conception and practice of Gulf security, one which rests on inclusion and not exclusion. Total security is an illusion, of course. But acting positively to transform potential threats into partners and basing policy on the participation of all sectors of Saudi society is the best option Saudi Arabia has.

STONEHILL COLLEGE

Notes

Acknowledgements

The author wishes to thank
Dr Yezid Sayigh for his detailed
comments on various drafts of
this paper and the Saudi
Committee for the Development
of International Trade, Council of
Saudi Chambers of Commerce
and Industry, for facilitating his
visit to Saudi Arabia.

All online material was accessible
on 1 June 2002

Introduction

1 Use of the term 'the Gulf' is
   meant to be neutral. Iranians
   are adamant that the body of
   water they share should be
   called 'the Persian Gulf', while
   Arabs are equally insistent that
   the name should be 'the
   Arabian Gulf'.
2 The Gulf Cooperation Council
   was formed in 1981 with six
   members: Saudi Arabia,
   Kuwait, Bahrain, Qatar, the
   United Arab Emirates (UAE)
   and Oman.
3 Monthly survey of oil
   production for December 2001,
   Reuters, 7 January 2002.
4 US Department of Energy, Energy
   Information Administration,
   International Energy Annual 2000
   (April 2002), as posted at
   www.eia.doe.gov/iea.
5 US White House, *Report of the
   National Energy Policy
   Development Group*
   (Washington, May 2001), p. 8–4
   (also posted online at
   www.whitehouse.gov/energy).
6 *BP AMOCO Statistical Review of
   World Energy 2001* (June 2001), p. 4.
7 Saudi Arabia Ministry of Oil and
   Mineral Resources, 'Direction of
   Crude Oil Exports 1981–1998'
   (online at
   http://www.mopm.gov.sa/
   html/en/s_tables/energy-st-
   9_e_2000.html). Other regions
   of the world constitute only
   minor destinations.
8 The Kingdom reckons its excess
   capacity at roughly 2 mbd.
   Information received by author
   in Saudi Arabia, February 2001.
9 Information received in Saudi
   Arabia, February 2001.

Chapter 1

1 Former head of Saudi intelligence Prince Turki al-Faisal Al Saud told American television on 3 February 2002 that Saudi Arabia had been pushing the United States to help internal Iraqi forces to overthrow Saddam since 1999, but he warned that an invasion of Iraq would be counterproductive. *Associated Press* (AP), 3 February 2002.

2 The Saudi diplomat Muhammad Khilawi, who sought political asylum in the United States in 1994, claimed to have documents alleging that Saudi Arabia had bankrolled Pakistan's bomb project since the 1970s, and that the two countries also signed a pact that provided for Pakistani use of its nuclear arsenal against any country attacking the Kingdom with nuclear weapons. *Sunday Times* (London), 24 July 1994. After Prince Sultan visited Pakistan's Kahuta nuclear facilities in May 1999, reports of Saudi intention to acquire nuclear weapons from Pakistan were swiftly denied by both countries. *Reuters*, 5 and 6 August 1999.

3 Members of ruling families throughout the Gulf often go to Pakistan to hunt and many have built residences there. One example of the special privileges these individuals receive occurred in 1994 when the press reported that Pakistan provided special permits so they could hunt the nearly extinct *houbara* bustard in Baluchistan. *Reuters*, 8 December 1994.

4 *Reuters*, 8 June and 25 and 27 October 1998; *Agence France-Presse* (AFP), 26 October 1998.

5 *Reuters*, 25, 26 and 27 October 1999.

6 AP, 10 December 2000. Musharraf visited Saudi Arabia a few months later to perform the *haj* (the Islamic pilgrimage) as well as to conduct talks with Saudi leaders. *Reuters*, 28 February 2001.

7 This may not have included some 3,000 pilots and technicians seconded under other programmes or recruited privately. *Economist*, 21 March and 12 December 1987; *Washington Post*, 28 November 1987; and US Foreign Broadcast and Information Service (FBIS), Middle East and North Africa (MENA), 3 December 1987, from the *Saudi Press Agency* (SPA), Riyadh, 2 December 1987.

8 FBIS MENA, 23 August 1988, from the Islamabad Domestic Service in Urdu, 22 August 1988; FBIS MENA, 31 August 1988, from the Islamic Republic of Iran News Agency, Tehran, in English, 29 August 1988.

9 It was alleged during the 1999 Kargil crisis that the Saudis persuaded Pakistan to withdraw its forces behind the Line of Control. *The Hindu*, 9 July 1999.

10 As of 1988, the Saudi government announced it had donated 445m Saudi riyals (approximately $120m) in aid to Afghanistan, although this figure appeared to refer to humanitarian aid only. FBIS MENA, 6 January 1988, from SPA, 4 January 1988.

11 One scholar estimates that about 12,000 young Saudis went to Afghanistan and that perhaps 5,000 of these were properly trained and saw combat.

Gwenn Okruhlik, 'Understanding Political Dissent in Saudi Arabia', *MERIP Press Information Note*, no. 73 (24 October 2001).

[12] *Middle East Economic Digest* (MEED), 26 March 1993; Saudi Arabian Embassy, Washington DC, *Newsletter*, April 1993.

[13] Riyadh's motivation for recognising the Taliban government appeared to be the furtherance of a viable central government in Afghanistan after years of anarchy. A newspaper report claimed 'Saudi Arabia's major charity' (unnamed) provided an estimated $2m annually in aid to Afghanistan and funded two universities, six health clinics, and supported 4,000 orphans. *Washington Post*, 15 October 2001. Why did the Kingdom fail to sever relations with the Taliban regime after the closeness of its relationship with bin Laden became clear? As Prince Turki al-Faisal, the head of Saudi intelligence until October 2001, explained it to an American reporter, he had reached agreement with Taliban leader Mullah Muhammad Omar that Osama bin Laden would be surrendered. But Omar reneged after the 1998 bombings of the American embassies in Kenya and Tanzania. Prince Turki said that the Kingdom had maintained minimal relations with the Taliban despite bin Laden's apparent involvement in the bombings in order to 'leave a door open' for a Taliban change of heart. *New York Times*, 27 December 2001. Prince Turki said in a later interview that the Kingdom did not break off

relations with the Taliban after they reneged on their promise to hand over bin Laden because 'we wanted at least to leave some tenuous link with them in case we needed to talk to them'. AP, 12 February 2002.

[14] The Kingdom announced on 22 September 1998 it was recalling its *chargé d'affaires* from Afghanistan and had asked the Afghan *chargé d'affaires* to leave Riyadh 'in keeping with national interests'. *Reuters*, 22 September 1998. Some sources contend that the Saudis actually were content to leave Osama in Afghanistan, given his earlier and allegedly continuing relationship with Saudi intelligence. See, *inter alia*, Ahmad Rashid, 'The Taliban: Exporting Extremism', *Foreign Affairs*, vol. 78, no. 6 (November–December 1999), p. 35.

[15] *Reuters*, 1 May 2000.

[16] Quoted in *Washington Post*, 15 October 2001. At the same time, the United States seemed more concerned with containing Iran and apparently viewed the Sunni extremism of the Taliban as a useful counter. *Ibid*. Another prominent member of the Al Saud noted that 'when the Taliban took over, Saudi Arabia – and even the United States – saw them as a ray of hope. Having Taliban in power meant that there would be centralized government and complete control over the nation. We thought that we might be able to discuss matters with the Taliban. This was all done in coordination with the United States. So if there is any blame to be placed, it should not be on Saudi Arabia alone,

because the US was seriously involved as well. Saudi Arabia, Pakistan and the United Arab Emirates all maintained communication with the Taliban, because we hoped that we would be able to accomplish something with them in the future. As former head of Saudi intelligence, Prince Turki al-Faisal, has indicated, we had relations with the Taliban because there was hope that they would hand over bin Laden'. Interview with Prince al-Walid bin Talal in *Middle East Insight* (January–February 2002).

17 Saudi Foreign Minister Prince Saud al-Faisal told reporters on 26 September 2001 that 'it is the duty of all of us to stand against the perpetrators of those abhorrent acts in the United States', but added that the money spent on a military campaign could be better used for aid for Afghanistan and that, if the United States was not careful with its first military strike, it could have a catastrophic effect. *Reuters*, 26 September 2001. Saudi disquiet was echoed elsewhere in the Gulf. The Saudi Minister of the Interior, Prince Nayif bin Abd al-Aziz, subsequently told reporters on 14 October that 'We had hoped that the United States would have been able to extract the terrorists in Afghanistan without resorting to what has happened, because there are innocents who have no guilt, and the people of Afghanistan as a whole have no responsibility for [attacks on the US] ... This situation does not please us at all, but that doesn't mean in any way that we won't fight with all our efforts to

uproot terrorism.' AP and *Reuters*, 15 October 2001. At the time of writing, the United States government still had not released any hard evidence of the guilt of Osama bin Laden and al-Qaeda in the 11 September hijackings, although a videotape of Osama's meeting with another 'Arab Afghan' from Saudi Arabia, discovered in the aftermath of the American attack on Afghanistan and released by the US Department of Defence on 13 December 2001, appeared to 'prove' guilt. *Washington Post*, 13 December 2001. The poor quality of the tape and various internal inconsistencies, along with its release by the American government, however, led many Muslims to doubt its veracity. Saudi dissident cleric Sheikh Hamud bin Uqla al-Shu'aybi was quoted as claiming that 'This is a dubbed tape and is not real at all'. *Reuters*, 16 December 2001. But the Saudi government had no doubts, as shown by the statement of the Saudi Ambassador to the US, Prince Bandar bin Sultan, who announced that it 'displays the cruel and inhumane face of a murderous criminal who has no respect for the sanctity of human life'. *Ibid*. Early reports that the Saudi visiting bin Laden and speaking on the videotape was a religious scholar were incorrect, and Saudi sources soon identified him as Khalid Awdah Muhammad al-Harbi, a legless 'Arab Afghan' who had also fought in Bosnia and Chechnya. *Reuters*, 16 December 2001; *Washington Post*, 17 December 2001.

18 *Reuters*, 19 and 21 January 2002.

19 This does not mean that the desire for GCC–Egyptian cooperation is dead. For example, the Kuwaiti Minister of Defence Sheikh Jabir al-Hamad Al Sabah told a Kuwaiti newspaper on 9 July 2001 that Egypt 'could directly participate in implementing the joint Gulf defence pact' and there was some speculation that Egypt could be linked to GCC command and control operations. *Reuters*, 9 July 2001.

20 *Reuters*, 4 December 2000. In March 2001, the Saudi government announced that it had given $2.37bn in aid to the Palestinians since 1991. *Reuters*, 20 March 2001.

21 One could posit that problems between the two countries date back to the war they fought in 1934, when Saudi forces took control of the provinces of Asir, Najran and Jizan.

22 Although the Saudis were pressured to withdraw in 1955, their claims to Buraimi, also known within the UAE as al-Ayn, were not dropped until border settlements were reached with Abu Dhabi in 1974 and Oman in 1990.

23 These figures are drawn from the International Institute for Strategic Studies, *The Military Balance 2001–2002* (London, 2001).

24 *Ibid.* The figures for the other states are: Bahrain, 11,000 personnel and $444m expenditure; Kuwait, 15,500 and $3.3bn; Oman, 43,400 and $1.7bn; Qatar, 12,330 and $1.4bn; and the UAE, 65,000 and $3.4bn.

25 J.E. Peterson, *Defending Arabia* (London: Croom Helm, 1986),
p. 151.

26 Anthony H. Cordesman, *The Gulf and Transition: US Policy Ten Years After the Gulf War* (Washington DC: Center for Strategic and International Studies, working draft, October 2000; online at http://www.csis.org/burke/gulf/index.htm, p. 73; *The Military Balance 2001–2002*, pp. 152–3. See also the draft chapters on all the Saudi Services by Cordesman in the 'Saudi Arabia Enters the 21st Century Project', Center for Strategic and International Studies, draft dated 9 January 2002, online at http://www.csis.org/burke/saudi21/index.htm

27 Peterson, *Defending Arabia*, p. 158; Cordesman, *The Gulf and Transition*, p. 74; and *The Military Balance 2001–2002*, pp. 152–3.

28 US Library of Congress, Federal Research Division, *Country Study on Saudi Arabia* (1992), online at http://lcweb2.loc.gov/frd/cs/satoc.html; Anthony H. Cordesman, 'Saudi Arabia Enters the 21st Century Project'; *The Military Balance 2001–2002*, p. 153.

29 Peterson, *Defending Arabia*, p. 157; Cordesman, *The Gulf and Transition*, p. 73; *The Military Balance 2001–2002*, pp. 152–3; and information received in Saudi Arabia, February 2001. The SANG, and not the army, repulsed Iraqi forces during the Battle of al-Khafji in the run-up to the Kuwait War. Contrary to widespread belief, the SANG does not provide security for the Royal Family, apart from the Heir Apparent, Prince Abdullah, who is the SANG commander.

[30] Information received in Saudi Arabia, February 2001.

[31] *The Military Balance 2001–2002*, p. 153; Anthony H. Cordesman, 'Saudi Arabia Enters the 21st Century Project'.

[32] The Soviet Union had been the first country to recognise Saudi Arabia in 1927, and Faisal bin Abd al-Aziz (later to become king) had actually visited the Soviet state in 1932 before relations lapsed in 1938.

[33] Fouad al-Farsy, *Modernity and Tradition: The Saudi Equation* (London: Kegan Paul International, 1990), p. 294.

[34] These organisations were created in the 1960s and early 1970s largely at the insistence of King Faisal, a man of very strong religious views.

[35] US Assistant Secretary of Commerce William Lach was quoted in late 2001 as estimating that Saudi investments in the US totalled approximately $500bn. In addition, the Kingdom was one of the US's biggest markets with more than $4bn in imports from the US in 2000. *Gulf News* (Dubai), 6 November 2001.

[36] On 21 June 2001 an American grand jury indicted 13 Saudis and a Lebanese for the bombing at the al-Khubar Towers. At a press conference in Washington the same day US Attorney General John Ashcroft alleged that those indicted were members of Saudi Hizbollah supported and directed by officials of the Iranian government. The timing of the indictments was governed by the imminent expiry of the statute of limitations on the crime, as well as by FBI director Louis Freeh's impending retirement. Iran immediately denied the allegations. AP, 22 June 2001. The following day, the Saudi Minister of the Interior, Prince Nayif bin Abd al-Aziz, told a Saudi newspaper that the Kingdom had not been given any advance warning of the step, maintained that trials must take place before Saudi judges, and averred there would be no extradition to the United States for crimes committed on Saudi soil. He also said that all but two Saudis and one Lebanese (identities not given) were in custody in Saudi Arabia. AP, 23 June 2001. There remains considerable doubt over the actual existence of a 'Saudi Hizbollah', and the indictment provided no clear evidence regarding Iranian involvement. Prince Nayif confirmed in an interview on 30 June that 11 of the 13 Saudis indicted were in Saudi prisons but reiterated that they would never be extradited. He also hinted that the trial of the 11 would begin soon. *New York Times*, 2 July 2001. The case had been marked by acrimony on both sides. The United States complained that the FBI were not given free access to detained suspects and the Saudi authorities failed to share all their information. From the Saudi point of view, the Clinton administration also withheld information, failed to keep the Saudis informed of American steps regarding the case, and the FBI acted arrogantly in the Kingdom (see Chapter 3, note 9, for similar reports on FBI attitudes in Yemen). A gossipy account of the case was published by Elsa Walsh, 'Louis

Freeh's Last Case', *New Yorker*, 14 May 2001. The text of the indictments has been posted in http://news.findlaw.com/cnn/docs/khobar/khobarindict61901.pdf.

[37] Richard F. Grimmett, *Conventional Arms Transfers to Developing Nations, 1993–2000* (Washington DC: Library of Congress, Congressional Research Service, 16 August 2001; Report RL31083), p. 59. Saudi Arabia received the largest delivery of arms by value amongst developing countries during this period. *Ibid.*

[38] Alfred B. Prados, *Saudi Arabia: Post-War Issues and US Relations* (Washington DC: Library of Congress, Congressional Research Service, 1 November 2001, Issue Brief 93113), p. 5.

[39] Information received in Saudi Arabia, February 2001.

[40] Other European deliveries over the same period totalled $7bn while Russian, Chinese and other deliveries totalled only $100m. Grimmett, *Conventional Arms Transfers*, p. 58.

[41] US State Department, Bureau of Arms Control, *World Military Expenditures and Arms Transfers 1998* (April 2000), online at http://www.state.gov/www/global/arms/bureau_ac/wmeat98/wmeat98.html, pp. 40–41.

[42] It was widely believed that the proposal never got off the ground because of Saudi opposition on the grounds that better-trained and motivated Omanis would provide a disproportionately large share of the force's personnel. On the other hand, it can be argued that the Saudis would retain

command and control functions, as they do for the present Peninsula Shield Force, and this would be the most important element in an effective force.

Chapter 2

[1] On the subject of succession in Saudi Arabia and the GCC, see Joseph A. Kechichian, *Succession in Saudi Arabia* (New York: Palgrave, 2001); J.E. Peterson, 'Succession in the States of the Gulf Cooperation Council', *Washington Quarterly*, vol. 24, no. 4 (Autumn 2001), pp. 173–86, and Peterson, 'The Nature of Succession in the Gulf', *Middle East Journal*, vol. 55, no. 4 (Autumn 2001), pp. 580–601.

[2] However, according to an unnamed American administration official, a Saudi intelligence survey in mid-October 2001 was said to have revealed that 95% of educated Saudis between the ages of 25 and 41 supported the cause of Osama bin Laden. *New York Times*, 27 January 2002.

[3] World Bank, *World Development Indicators (2000)* (online at http://www.worldbank.org/data/wdi2000/index.htm); information received in Saudi Arabia, February 2001.

[4] US Embassy, Riyadh, 'Saudi Arabia: 2001 Economic Trends' (online, http://usembassy.state.gov/riyadh/wwwhet01.html).

[5] World Bank, *World Development Indicators (2000)* (online).

[6] Saleh Abdullah Malik, 'Rural Migration and Urban Growth in Riyadh, Saudi Arabia' (Ph.D. dissertation, University of Michigan, 1973), p. 8; Sanaa Abd

El-Hamid Kaoud, 'Demographic
Developments in Saudi Arabia
During the Present Century'
(Ph.D. thesis, City University,
London, 1979), p. 32;
information received in Saudi
Arabia, February 2001.

7 The changing nature of social
relations, including often
pessimistic outlooks for the
future, is well illustrated in the
series of interviews conducted
by Mai Yamani with members
of Saudi Arabia's younger
generation in her *Changed
Identities: The Challenge of the
New Generation in Saudi Arabia*
(London: Royal Institute of
International Affairs, 2000).

8 The emergence of a middle class
in the GCC states has been
analysed in J.E. Peterson,
'Change and Continuity in Arab
Gulf Society', in Charles Davies
(ed.), *After the War: Iraq, Iran
and the Arab Gulf* (Chichester:
Carden, for the University of
Exeter Centre for Arab Gulf
Studies, 1990), pp. 287–312.

9 Saudi Arabia, Ministry of
Planning, *Achievements of the
Development Plans 1390–1420
(1970–2000)* (Riyadh, 2000), p. 160.

10 Information received in Saudi
Arabia, February 2001.

11 Information received in Saudi
Arabia, 1986, 1988 and February
2001. Of course, students in
secular universities and other
vocational institutes, as well as in
Western educational institutions,
may also develop Islamist
inclinations. Although
information on the 11 September
hijackers is sketchy, it appears
that some at least received some
education beyond secondary-
school level in disciplines not
related to Islamic teaching. It
should be remembered, too, that

Osama bin Laden was trained as
an engineer.

12 The Ikhwan are discussed
below.

13 In fact, an earlier, rudimentary,
consultative council had been
established for the Hijaz region
in the 1920s and expanded in
the 1950s with Najdi
representation. On the
background to the Saudi *Majlis
al-Shura*, see J.E. Peterson, *The
Arab Gulf States: Steps Toward
Political Participation* (New York:
Praeger, Washington: Center
for Strategic and International
Studies, 1988; Washington
Papers, no. 131), pp. 112–15.

14 A study on the second *majlis*
noted that the membership held
47 doctorates and at least 44
master's degrees. Members
were drawn from all regions of
the country and included two
Shiite. R. Hrair Dekmejian,
'Saudi Arabia's Consultative
Council,' *Middle East Journal*, vol.
52, no. 2 (Spring 1998), p. 210.

15 Anthony H. Cordesman, 'Saudi
Military Forces and the Gulf'
(Washington DC: Center for
Strategic and International
Studies, 4 February 1999),
pp. 32–3.

16 Saudi arms transfer agreements
totalled $18.8bn for 1993–96, but
only $5.7bn for the 1997–2000
period. Grimmett, *Conventional
Arms Transfers*, p. 47.

17 *Achievements of the Development
Plans*, p. 218.

18 The attractions of joining the
Saudi security forces include
securing a job for life and
gaining valuable vocational
training and work discipline
which can be transferred later
to private-sector jobs.
Information received in Saudi
Arabia, February 2001.

[19] Information received in Saudi Arabia, February 2001. Much the same can be said for tribesmen from rural areas throughout the country. The hijacking of a Saudi airliner to Baghdad in 2000 was carried out by two Saudi security officers with strong tribal ties. *Ibid.* A similar hijacking took place in 1996 when three Saudis, apparently from the Bani Hilal tribe of Najd, hijacked an EgyptAir flight from Jeddah and forced it to fly to Libya; they claimed they had received a message from God about lifting the siege of Palestine and supporting Sudan. *Reuters*, 27 March 1996.

[20] As Brad Bourland, Chief Economist of the Saudi American Bank, has pointed out, Saudi Arabia has the largest economy in the Arab world, with a GDP in 2000 of approximately $170bn. But its economy remains smaller than that of the metropolitan area of Washington DC (approximately $200bn) and is dwarfed by the GDPs of France and the UK (at approximately $1.5 trillion) and the United States (about $9 trillion). Furthermore, he notes that for the last decade real GDP growth in the region has been only about 1% per year. Bourland, 'Opportunities and Constraints in Saudi Commercial and Economic Development', reproduced in 'GulfWire Perspectives', www.Arabialink.com.

[21] The US Embassy in Riyadh reported that per capita GDP in both Saudi Arabia and the US was about $28,600 in 1981. However, in 2000 US per capita GDP reached $36,645 while Saudi Arabia's had fallen below $8,000. Per capita GDP for 2001 was projected at less than $7,000. US Embassy, Riyadh, 'Saudi Arabia: 2001 Economic Trends' (online, http://usembassy.state.gov/riyadh/wwwhet01.html). These figures were confirmed by discussions in Saudi Arabia during February 2001.

[22] The Five-Year Development Plan for 2001–2005 forecasts that approximately one million Saudis will graduate from secondary school over the course of the plan, with some 400,000 of those going on to receive an undergraduate degree. Bourland, 'Opportunities and Constraints'.

[23] This is skilfully illustrated in Haya al-Mughni, *Women in Kuwait: The Politics of Gender*, 2nd ed. (London: Saqi Books, 2001).

Chapter 3

[1] *Oman News Agency* interview relayed by *Reuters*, 29 December 2001.

[2] *Reuters*, 30 December 2001. Prince Abdullah also condemned Israel's repression of Palestinians and asked rhetorically, 'Would the bloody oppression ... occur if Israel were confronted by a united Arab and Muslim nation?' *Ibid.*

[3] Poll published in *al-Qabas* (Kuwait) as reported by *Reuters*, 19 November 2001.

[4] But see Chapter 2, note 2.

[5] As the term Wahabi is more common, it is used in this work. Notwithstanding media usage, Wahabism is not a sect but a reformist movement within mainstream Sunni Islam, and Wahabis follow the Hanbali

school of jurisprudence, the
most conservative of the four
recognised schools in Sunni
Islam. As King Abd al-Aziz
explained in a 1929 speech in
Mecca, 'They call us the
"Wahabis" and they call our
creed a "Wahabi" one as if it were
a special one ... and this is an
extremely erroneous allegation
that has arisen from the false
propaganda launched by those
who had ill feelings as well as ill
intentions towards the
movement. We are not
proclaiming a new creed or a
new dogm'. Quoted in al-Farsy,
Modernity and Tradition, pp. 20–21.

6 The leader of the 1979 siege,
Juhayman al-Utaybi came from
a Najdi tribe with strong
Ikhwan ties and seems to have
seen his role in similar terms.
On the Ikhwan and the political
background to modern Saudi
Arabia, see, *inter alia*, John S.
Habib, *Ibn Sa'ud's Warriors of
Islam: The Ikhwan of Najd and
Their Role in the Creation of the
Sa'udi Kingdom, 1910–1930*
(Leiden: E.J. Brill, 1978), and
Christine Moss Helms, *The
Cohesion of Saudi Arabia:
Evolution of Political Identity*
(London: Croom Helm;
Baltimore: Johns Hopkins
University Press, 1981). On
Juhayman, see Joseph A.
Kechichian, 'Islamic Revivalism
and Change in Saudi Arabia:
Juhayman al-'Utaybi's "Letters"
to the Saudi People', *Muslim
World*, vol. 80, no. 1 (1990),
pp. 1–16.

7 Eventually, however, the
universities established
women's branches, thus
bringing female education at
university level back under the
control of the Ministry of
Higher Education.

8 There has also been a history of
opposition within the minority
Shiite community of the Eastern
Province but, for the most part,
this has been due to
discriminatory treatment rather
than religious extremism. The
Iranian Revolution in 1979 and
the outbreak of the Iran–Iraq
War in 1980 prompted some
younger Shiite to agitate for
greater Shiite freedom in an
Iran-inspired Islamist
framework, which then
provoked a severe government
response. It took several years
for Riyadh to seek to redress
the problem by funnelling aid
to Shiite areas and rebuilding
Shiite mosques.

9 The *Guardian* (London)
reported on 8 October 2001 that
Sheikh Hamud bin Uqla al-
Shu'aybi issued a *fatwa*
(religious legal opinion)
supposedly declaring that
'Whoever supports the infidel
against Muslims is considered
an infidel ... it is a duty to wage
jihad on anyone who attacks
Afghanistan'. Similar
declarations were issued by two
other dissidents, Sulayman
Alwan and Ali Khudayr.
Shu'aybi died in Buraydah of a
heart attack on 19 January 2002.
AP, 19 January 2002.

10 On bin Laden's background, see
inter alia US Department of
State, 'Factsheet on Usama bin
Laden', 14 August 1996; Madawi
Al-Rasheed, 'Saudi Arabia's
Islamic Opposition', *Current
History*, vol. 95, no. 597 (January
1996), pp. 18 and 20; and
Mamoun Fandy, *Saudi Arabia
and the Politics of Dissent* (New
York: St Martin's Press and
Basingstoke: Macmillan, 1999),

p. 181.

11 *Reuters* and AP, 22 April 1996; FBIS MENA, 31 May 1996, from SPA 31 May 1996. Masari's apparent statement that the US soldiers killed in the bomb attack constituted a legitimate target sparked official Saudi outrage and an attempt by the British government to deport him to the Caribbean. Masari claimed he had been misquoted and successfully petitioned the courts to stay the deportation order. *Reuters*, 16 November 1995, 6 January 1996 and 5 March 1996. A dispute shortly afterward between Masari and his collaborator Sa'd al-Faqih led to the latter's formation of a separate group, the Movement for Islamic Reform. UPI, 12 March 1996.

12 The 19 hijackers were named by the FBI on 27 September 2001 as: (1) Khalid Almihdhar, (2) Majed Moqed, (3) Nawwaf Alhazmi, (4) Salem Alhazmi, (5) Hani Hanjour, (6) Satam M.A. Al Suqami, (7) Waleed M. Alshehri, (8) Wail M. Alshehri, (9) Mohamed Atta, (10) Abdulaziz Alomari (11) Marwan Al-Shehhi, (12) Fayez Rashid Ahmad Hasan Al Qadi Banihammad, (13) Ahmad Alghamdi, (14) Hamzah Alghamdi, (15) Mohand Alshehri, (16) Said Alghamdi, (17) Ahmad Ibrahim A. Al Haznawi, (18) Ahmad Alnami and (19) Ziad Samir Jarrah. (The names are given here in their original, sometimes garbled, form, including inconsistent transliteration). US Federal Bureau of Investigation, National Press Office, 27 September, 2001, http://www.fbi.gov/pressrel/

pressrel01/092701hjpic.htm. The Saudis come from such areas as Bani Ghamid (in the western mountains), Jizan (on the Red Sea coast), Asir and Najran (in the south on the border with Yemen), a village near Medina and the city of Taif (both in the important western province of Hijaz), and the northern rural region near Jordan. One report claimed that they included the brother of a police commander, the son of a tribal sheikh, the son of a wealthy businessman, two teachers and three law graduates. *The Sunday Times* (London), 28 October 2001; *Boston Globe*, 3 March 2002.

13 *Arab News* (Jeddah), 14 December 2001, citing *Ukaz* (Jeddah).

14 An unnamed Saudi intelligence official was said to have estimated that 200–1,000 Saudis were involved in 2001 fighting in Afghanistan. *Washington Post*, 17 December 2001. The Saudi ambassador to Pakistan told a Saudi newspaper that some 140 Arab families, including Saudis but excluding men, were stuck on the Afghan–Pakistani border, and that the Kingdom was attempting to identify them and secure the Saudis' return to the Kingdom. BBC Monitoring Global Newsline, *al-Watan* (Abha), 17 December 2001. About the same time, the Americans claimed to have captured a Saudi associated with the proscribed Wafa Humanitarian Organisation, who, they said, was a high-ranking member of al-Qaeda. *New York Times*, 18 December 2001. Pakistani Minister of the Interior Moinuddin Haidar told *Ukaz* (Jeddah) that US and

Pakistani interrogators were questioning about 240 Saudis captured inside Pakistan after fleeing Afghanistan, and that any with links to al-Qaeda would be turned over to the FBI. Cited by *Reuters*, 5 January 2002. Saudi nationals comprised at least two of the five men identified by the FBI as major al-Qaeda suspects from a videotape recovered in Afghanistan. AP, 19 January 2002. On 28 January 2002, Saudi Minister of the Interior Prince Nayif said that about 100 Saudis were among the prisoners held by the United States at its Guantanamo base in Cuba, adding that the Kingdom wished the US to hand them over to Riyadh. *Reuters*, 28 January 2002.

15 The marginality of Osama in Saudi society (as the son of a Yemeni immigrant and thus not a true Saudi in the eyes of many) may also have been a factor in the development of his receptivity to extremism. Mamoun Fandy, in *Saudi Arabia and the Politics of Dissent*, discusses the role of marginality in producing dissident religious activists in the tightly cohesive society of the Kingdom.

16 President's Address to a Joint Session of Congress, 20 September 2001, online at http://www.whitehouse.gov/news/releases/2001/09/20010920-8.html.

17 The FBI refused to give details of the thousands of individuals it had detained. Some 50 or more men apparently of Saudi nationality were reported to be on the bureau's terrorist watch list. *Washington Post*, 15 October 2001. The release of the first 22

Saudis amongst the detainees, and then of another 12, was announced by the Saudi ambassador to the US, Prince Bandar bin Sultan, who said that most of the Saudis held in the US had been detained for violating immigration laws, traffic laws, or other minor offences. *Reuters*, 4 January 2002, citing SPA. The Saudi Embassy in Washington added that it had been contacted by over 200 Saudi families seeking information on missing relatives. *Reuters*, 14 January 2002. The embassy further announced on 31 January 2002 that another 10 prisoners had been released, and 23 more were still being held. *Arab News* (Jeddah), 1 February 2002. The comments and allegations of mistreatment of some of those released can be found in *Arab News* (Jeddah), 7 January 2002, and *Reuters*, 14 January 2002. An estimated 5,000 or more men, many of them Arabs, had been taken into custody for investigation. *Reuters*, 4 January 2002.

18 Amnesty International was quoted in the *Financial Times* (30 October 2001) as remarking 'These are exceptional times ... But public officials must not take exception to their commitments to protect human rights and the rule of law. The United States will not be well served if it erodes its own values in the name of justice.'

19 Even though Dr al-Badr al-Hazmi was completely cleared, released and allowed to take his family back to Saudi Arabia, when he flew back to the US he discovered that his visa had been cancelled without his

knowledge. He was forced to return to Saudi Arabia a second time and obtain a new visa there. AP, 8 January 2002.

[20] AFP, 28 December 2001. The airline claimed his paperwork was improper and that he was abusive. The agent, however, continued to deny the accusations and filed complaints with appropriate government agencies. *Washington Post*, 13 January 2002.

[21] The individual was Rep. Darrell Issa (California Republican). AP, 26 October 2001.

[22] See above, Chapter 3, note 17.

[23] Televised comment by Senator John McCain (Arizona Republican), reported in MEED, 29 October 2001. On the same programme, Senator Joseph Lieberman (Connecticut Democrat) said the Saudis 'have satisfied their extremists within their own societies ... [and] also financed some of these organisations' and declared that the United States 'can't tolerate a nation like the Saudis ... to promulgate that hatred'. *Washington Post*, 6 November 2001.

[24] Senator Joseph Biden (Delaware Democrat) in remarks at the Council on Foreign Relations. *Reuters*, 23 October 2001.

[25] Statement to reporters by Senator Carl Levin (Michigan Democrat) on 15 January 2002. Another congressman and chairman of the House Intelligence Committee, Porter J. Goss (Florida Democrat) claimed that 'It's pretty tyrannical there'. *New York Times*, 16 January 2002.

[26] AP, 8 January 2002.

[27] For example, a later report in the *Washington Post* said that two suspected al-Qaeda members were arrested in Bahrain shortly after the attacks and sent to Saudi Arabia. Using information they provided, Saudi authorities arrested six more al-Qaeda members and provided the FBI and CIA with limited access to them. *International Herald Tribune*, 23 November 2001. Western diplomats in Riyadh were said to have confirmed that the Saudi authorities had rounded up about 400 people linked to al-Qaeda after the September attacks, although a few hundred had already left for Afghanistan. *Reuters*, 5 January 2002. Another report said that the Saudi government had asked the other GCC states to provide it with photocopies of passports of Saudis arriving from countries other than the Kingdom in an attempt to prevent Saudis disguising their return from Pakistan or Afghanistan. BBC Monitoring Global Newsline, *al-Rayah* (Doha) website, 10 January 2002.

[28] As late as November, the Saudis continued to complain that the US had provided no evidence to back their demands for action against individuals and institutions and had not clarified the identities of those on the list. One anonymous Saudi official was quoted as saying 'When [the Americans] ask us to do something, we say, "Give us the evidence". That's when they accuse us of helping the terrorists'. *New York Times*, 27 November 2001. One Saudi businessman, accused by the US Treasury Department of channelling money to al-Qaeda, filed suit in a British court to

stop the freezing of his assets in that country. *Ibid.* A high-level US delegation, composed of representatives from the Treasury, FBI, State Department and National Security Council, arrived in the Kingdom on 13 December 2001 to discuss the freezing of assets of suspected individuals and Islamic charities. These discussions apparently helped to sharpen identification of suspected culprits and enhanced cooperation. *Reuters,* 23 January 2002. In subsequent actions, Saudi officials announced action would be taken against the owners of 150 bank accounts allegedly involved in money-laundering activities (*Arab News* [Jeddah], 5 February 2002) and that four bank accounts linked to al-Qaeda had been frozen (AP, 7 February 2002). Some 230 charitable organisations exist in the Kingdom, with offices and representatives in about 55 countries, and during 2001 they collected more than one billion Saudi riyals (about $275m) from businessmen, members of charities, *zakat* (the Islamic alms tax) and returns on investments. *Arab News* (Jeddah), 14 December 2001.

29 The *Washington Post*, correcting its earlier story of 22 September 2001, reported on 28 September that Saudi Arabia would allow US troops and aircraft stationed in the Kingdom to participate in military action in Afghanistan. Secretary of State Colin Powell told a television interviewer on 23 September that the original *Washington Post* article was 'incorrect' in saying that he had protested any Saudi denial and added that the Saudis 'have

been very responsive to all of the requests we have placed on them' (US Department of State transcript of the interview, 23 September 2001, online at http://usinfo.state.gov/topical/pol/terror/01092400.htm), and an unidentified senior administration official said that the US Central Command was operating its command and control centre at the Prince Sultan base with 200 Americans working to coordinate the build-up of air power around Afghanistan (*Stars and Stripes,* 26 September 2001). Saudi Foreign Minister Prince Saud al-Faisal also denied the report on 26 September 2001, remarking 'You had the denial of the Americans about the truth of that article. Now you have the denial of the Saudis'. *Reuters,* 26 September 2001.

30 See, for example, President Bush's comment during a telephone call with Prince Abdullah that 'press articles citing differences between the United States and Saudi Arabia are simply incorrect' (relayed by White House Press Secretary Ari Fleischer during press briefing on 25 October 2001, online at http://www.whitehouse.gov/news/releases/2001/10/20011025-5.html). An unnamed US government official told *Reuters* (6 December 2001) that the two governments had a 'positive, good dialogue'; and White House Chief of Staff Andrew Card commented after Saudi Foreign Minister Prince Saud al-Faisal's meeting with President Bush that the Saudis 'have been very cooperative. The President

expressed his appreciation' (*Washington Post*, 8 December 2001). Assistant Secretary of State William Burns remarked that 'the United States relationship with Saudi Arabia is a very strong relationship, including in security' (*Reuters* 10 December 2001); and the White House announced that President Bush had telephoned Prince Abdullah to discuss the war on terrorism and 'thanked Saudi Arabia for their friendship, cooperation and help.' (*Reuters*, 14 January 2002).

[31] *Washington Post*, 18 January 2002. *The Economist* (26 January 2002) identified the source of this idea as Prince Talal bin Abd al-Aziz, a former minister, former exile and ruling family member, and opined that the 'leak' was for local consumption. Undeterred by US and Saudi denials, the *Washington Post* published an editorial (20 January 2002) seemingly endorsing the removal of troops. The *Guardian* (London, 27 March 2002), citing Saudi dissidents, reported that US Air Force vehicles had been observed moving equipment from Prince Sultan air base to al-Udayd air base in Qatar. The American Central Command admitted that communications and computer equipment was being moved but stressed it was to improve 'operational flexibility' of its forces in the region and did not constitute abandonment of Saudi facilities, relocation of its Gulf headquarters, or indicate an imminent attack on Iraq. *Reuters* and AP, 27 March 2002.

[32] Poll carried out by Dr. James J. Zogby, President, Arab American Institute, 24 December 2001, reprinted in *GulfWire*, 24 December. Plans for a massive media campaign in the West to improve public opinion regarding the Arab world were shelved at the GCC summit in Muscat (30–31 December 2001). *Reuters*, 31 December 2001.

[33] *The Economist*, 6–13 March 1999.

[34] With petrol prices in the United States near $1 a gallon (compared to about $4 in much of Europe) and ownership of petrol-greedy four-wheel-drive vehicles steadily increasing, it is hard to fathom the indignant belief of American consumers that they are being gouged.

[35] Prince Abdullah told a visiting American delegation in February 2001 that 'Israel must realize an important point: forty years ago you could not find any Arab who would shake hands with an Israeli. Today, as a result of the peace process and preparation by their leaders, it is possible for the public to accept the principle of co-existence and stability for both sides. Israel must not continue to ignore this change in attitude brought about by the peace process, and must not miss the opportunity to resolve one of the longest-running conflicts of modern times. If the opportunity is missed, the consequences will be negative'. Personal information received in Saudi Arabia, February 2001. A year later, Prince Abdullah told an American newspaper that he had drafted a speech for an Arab summit calling for 'Full withdrawal from all the occupied territories, in accord

with United Nations resolutions, including Jerusalem, for full normalization of relations' but that 'I changed my mind about delivering it when Sharon took the violence, and the oppression, to an unprecedented level'. *New York Times*, 17 February 2002.

[36] In the weeks after the bombing of the destroyer in Aden Harbour in October 2000, it was reported that the FBI flew its investigators by helicopter into Aden from a ship offshore without even filing a flight plan on at least one occasion. AFP, 2 November 2000. The FBI's in-country relations deteriorated so greatly that the American Ambassador in Sana'a, Barbara Bodine, banned the head of the FBI's investigation team, John O'Neill, from setting foot in Yemen. *New York Times*, 6 July 2001; *Washington Post*, 7 July 2001. O'Neill retired from the FBI in August 2001 and, ironically, took up a new job as director of security for the World Trade Center two weeks before the attacks, in which he was killed. CNN.com, 12 September 2001 (online at http://www.cnn.com/2001/US/09/12/victim.wtc.security).

[37] For details of this indictment, Chapter 1, note 36.

[38] Recent statistics show that in AH 1419–1420 (1997–8), there were 2,369,000 female students in Saudi Arabia, compared to 2,405,000 males, and that 21,721 women finished their higher education that year, compared to 21,229 men. *Achievements of the Development Plans*, pp. 308, 310, 317, 320.

[39] For more than a year, there has been some concern amongst analysts in the United States government that the Al Saud may be on the verge of losing control. Information received in Saudi Arabia and elsewhere, 2001. The *Boston Globe* reported on 5 March 2002 that a US Central Intelligence Agency 'National Intelligence Estimate' prepared on Saudi Arabia in autumn 2002 apparently described the Al Saud regime as an 'anachronism', 'isolated' and 'inherently fragile'.

[40] Saudi caution was echoed by pronouncements by senior religious figures in the Kingdom. Sheikh Abd al-Rahman al-Sudays told worshippers during the Friday *khutbah* (sermon) at the Great Mosque in Mecca on 28 September 2001 that 'It would be a grave calamity when the followers of this phenomenon [of terrorism] use religion as a camouflage, because true Islam stands innocent from all that', adding that Muslims should not 'mix up the concepts of real terrorism and legitimate *jihad* (religious struggle)'. *Reuters*, 28 September 2001. Prince Nayif bin Abd al-Aziz, the Minister of the Interior, told a gathering of Saudi security officers to 'Be vigilant and reject those who try to impair security in the name of Islam', adding 'Do not forget that those who abused your country are those sitting in their caves and holes and are sorrowfully associated with Islam, and Islam stands aloft from them'. *Reuters*, 17 October 2001.

[41] Heir Apparent Prince Abdullah announced in late November

2001 that civil identity cards would soon be issued to women (*Arab News*, 27 November 2001, citing *al-Hayat*, 26 November) and the first several thousand cards were issued soon after. AP, 5 December 2001; *Reuters*, 10 December 2001.

[42] See, for example, the comments of Prince al-Walid bin Talal, the prominent Saudi businessman and investor, in an interview that 'Inevitably what's going on in America will scare Saudis for sure ... not only from investing in America but in going to America. All Arab names are ruined in America right now. If an Arab goes there he is a liability, he is not welcome.' *Reuters*, 23 October 2001. One report said that at least 300 Saudi students returned home after 11 September, many of whom attributed their decision to harassment by officials and the American population. American consular officials admitted that the number of Saudi visa applications in late 2001 was running far below the 60,000 issued for the year up to October 2001. *New York Times*, 7 December 2001. Many of these, however, intended to return for the spring semester, although mostly without their families. Anecdotal evidence from travel agents in the Gulf suggested that many Saudis were changing travel plans for the Id al-Fitr end-of-Ramadan holiday from the US or Europe to such destinations as Beirut, Egypt, Morocco, Malaysia and India. *Gulf News* (Dubai), 12 December 2001. Other sources estimated that more than 40,000 Saudis would not be taking their holidays in the US during 2002. *Arab News* (Jeddah), 15 February 2002. Another report said that investment capital worth $24bn had been withdrawn back to Saudi Arabia between 11 September and the end of November. *Arab News*, 2 January 2002. Subsequent reports contradicted this, with Prince Abdullah bin Faisal bin Turki, Chairman of Saudi Arabian General Investment Authority, guessing that only about $4bn had returned, and at least one US bank claimed that there had been no withdrawal of US-based assets. *Reuters*, 25 January 2002.

[43] At the time of writing, an American attack on Iraq seemed to be just sabre-rattling. Still, President Bush's hint in mid-November that Iraq could be next if it did not allow the return of UN inspectors was followed in mid-December by the comment of National Security Adviser Condoleezza Rice to *al-Hayat* (London) that 'the world and Iraq will live better without Saddam Hussein in power' (cited by AFP, 20 December 2001) and the inclusion of Iraq in the 'evil axis' in President Bush's State of the Union address. More hints by senior administration figures followed in the first half of 2002, and a tour of the GCC states by US Vice-President Richard Cheney in March 2002 was said to have been an unsuccessful attempt to drum up support for an attack on Iraq.

[44] This was echoed in an interview given by Prince Turki al-Faisal, shortly after he stepped down as chief of Saudi intelligence. 'You target Saddam Hussein

and no one will boo or hiss or object', he was quoted as saying. 'But bombings like the ones we saw against Iraq in 1998, or like the ones we've seen now in Afghanistan, with so-called collateral bombings, when bombs hit innocent people, will have strong resonance and very bad implications for relations with the West'. *International Herald Tribune*, 22 November 2001.

[45] *Reuters*, 16 February 2002.

[46] Statement reproduced in 'GulfWire Voices of the Region', 4–10 June 2001, www.Arabialink.com. The voicing of Saudi displeasure with US support for Israel against the Palestinians prompted former President George Bush to telephone the Saudi Heir Apparent Prince Abdullah in late June to reassure him that his son, President George W. Bush, 'was going to do the right thing' in the Middle East. *New York Times*, 15 July 2001.

[47] WAM, 3 July 2001. Similar sentiments were expressed by Saudi Foreign Minister Prince Saud al-Faisal Al Saud on 5 September 2001, when he told a press conference in Amman that 'It is time especially for the United States to assume its responsibility and prevent Israeli aggression against the Arab world'. *Reuters*, 5 September 2001. The day before the 11 September attacks, the Saudi-owned newspaper *al-Sharq al-Awsat* reported that the issue had caused the Saudi government to put off the annual talks of the joint Saudi–US military committee in late August. *Reuters*, 10 September 2001.

[48] For example, Foreign Minister Prince Saud al-Faisal said on 9 November 2001 that the Saudi government was 'angrily frustrated' that the Bush administration had not initiated a new peace initiative and declared that President Bush could not become an 'honest broker' in the peace process until he met with Palestinian President Yasser Arafat. Bush refused to see Arafat on the same day, even though both were in New York for UN General Assembly meetings. *New York Times*, 9 November 2001.

Conclusions

[1] Examples of potential 'bridge-building' projects might be the inclusion of Iraq in the proposed Iran–Kuwait fresh-water pipeline and in the proposed Gulf gas grid or gas pipeline from Qatar to Kuwait, and greater Iraqi use of Kuwaiti territory for access to the Gulf. In early 2002, Kuwait announced it was creating a committee to promote development cooperation between Kuwait and Iran, including railway links between the Gulf and beyond to Central Asia. *Reuters*, 8 April 2002.

[2] For example, better Iran–UAE (and, especially, better Iran–GCC) relations might open the way for a face-saving compromise over the three islands of the Gulf claimed by the UAE but unilaterally occupied by Iran.

[3] Such efforts almost inevitably lead to enduring bitterness, as shown by the example of the

1975 Algiers Accord on the division of the Shatt al-Arab waterway between Iran and Iraq. Iraq's belief that it had been made to sign the accord under duress was one justification for the attack on Iran in 1980.

4 The powerful role of satellite television in disseminating information and ideas was clearly shown during the American war in Afghanistan, when Qatar's controversial Jazeera station, the only in-country television presence, broadcast information on the war and statements by Osama bin Laden throughout the Middle East.

5 While Israel may, *in extremis*, serve as a base for US force projection, it is a liability in political and financial terms for the US in the Middle East – and of course can play no positive role in a wider Islamic world stretching from Pakistan to Malaysia.

U 162 .A3 no.348

Peterson, John, 1947-

Saudi Arabia and the
  illusion of security

DATE DUE

NOV 1 4 2003			
MAR 1 0 2004			
MAY 1 4 2010			

GAYLORD   PRINTED IN U.S.A

DISCARDED BY

MACPHÁIDÍN LIBRARY

MACPHÁIDÍN LIBRARY
STONEHILL COLLEGE
EASTON, MASSACHUSETTS 02357